The New Centralism

Britain Out of Step in Europe?

The New Centralism

Britain Out of Step in Europe?

Edited by
Colin Crouch and David Marquand

Basil Blackwell

ISBN 0–631–16693–9

First published 1989

Basil Blackwell Ltd.
108 Cowley Road, Oxford, OX4 1JF, UK.

Basil Blackwell Inc.
3 Cambridge Center,
Cambridge, Ma. 02142, USA.

British Library Cataloguing in Publication Data and Library of Congress Cataloging in Publication Data applied for

Typeset by Hope Services (Abingdon) Ltd.
Printed in Great Britain by Whitstable Litho, Kent.

CONTENTS

FOREWORD

NOT least among the paradoxes of British politics in the 1980s is the way in which relations between central and local government have evolved in practice. Traditional Toryism saw local councils as independent repositories of political will, as barriers between a potentially overmighty state and a potentially vulnerable civil society. With a few exceptions, British socialists have traditionally looked to the central state to realise their purposes, if necessary—as in the creation of the National Health Service and the reorganisation of secondary education—by overriding local resistance. Yet in the last ten years a Conservative government, committed to a sweeping reduction in the role of the state and determined to break with the allegedly consensual practices of the post-war period, has accelerated the erosion of local government power which had been one of the most obvious features of that period. And one of the reasons is that in many inner-city areas left-wing socialists have deliberately sought to use local government as a mechanism for frustrating or even negating central government policies.

Rate-capping, the poll tax and the curtailment of local authority competence which has been a feature of a whole series of acts of parliament have all made local councils even more subordinate to central control than they were before. They have also reminded us how easily a British government with a majority at Westminster can change the balance of territorial power. A whole tier of local government—the Greater London Council and the metropolitan councils which were responsible for a number of local authority functions in the biggest conurbations—has been abolished, without prior inquiry or consultation, even though, at least in the case of the GLC, a clear majority of the public in the area concerned was opposed to abolition. But it would be wrong to suggest that this was a uniquely flagrant or outrageous usurpation on the part of the Thatcher government. The authorities which were summarily abolished by *fiat* of central government in the 1980s had been created in the 1960s and 1970s also by *fiat* of Conservative central government, albeit following some form of public enquiry and debate. And their creation had been accompanied by the equally summary abolition of a mass of much older authorities, with much deeper roots in British history.

Two other features of the Thatcher government's approach to the territorial constitution deserve attention as well. Local councils wishing to assist economic development in their areas have had a particularly discouraging experience, even though one might have thought that an attempt to help wealth creation rather than just act as conduits for

vii

public expenditure might have struck a supportive chord with Margaret Thatcher's government. Meanwhile, we have been reminded once again how intolerant Westminster and Whitehall are of any autonomous political expression by the non-English parts of the United Kingdom.

The authors in the first part of this volume address these aspects of what must now be seen as the extraordinary centralism of British government and politics. Tony Travers traces and analyses the various components of the destruction of local government powers. James Bulpitt offers a different perspective on the implications of the last decade for traditional British attitudes to the territorial constitution, stressing the continuities between this and earlier periods and suggesting, in effect, that *plus ça change, plus c'est la même chose*. Alan Harding examines the fate of attempts by British local councils to run urban economic development programmes; and Chris Harvie uses England's treatment of Scotland to draw some general conclusions about the character of the English state, both in earlier periods of history and in its current phase.

What are we to make of the picture they paint? What, in particular, are we to make of the paradox of determined state centralism in a government devoted to the free market and anxious to minimise state intervention in the economy? Two broad answers stand out. The first is that, as Andrew Gamble has suggested in his study of the Thatcher administrations *The Free Economy and the Strong State*[1], state centralism and new right economics may, in fact, go together. If the market is to reign supreme and not be subject to repeated political interference, then the political must be gathered into a tight, predictable, unit controlled by the friends of the free market. If it is dispersed in politically heterogeneous and variously located bundles, some of these may fall into the hands of enemies of the market; if that happens, as it did in a number of inner cities in the 1980s, the reign of market freedom will not dawn after all. That part of the new right case is logically coherent and not in itself contradictory, though it does at first sight imply contradictions with some of the other goals supposed to be achieved by increased reliance on the market: prevention of concentrations of power in a few hands, delegation of choice to the lowest possible levels, the promotion of variety.

Only at first sight, however. One of the central assumptions of the new right is that choice is maximised through the market, not through politics: that the frictionless, undistorted market is a realm of freedom and the polity a realm of domination, intimidation and manipulation. Grant that and it follows logically that the sphere of the political should be curtailed; one obvious way to do this is to limit the scope of subordinate political authorities. On new right assumptions, provided people have the chance to vote in national elections and to participate in

[1] Andrew Gamble, *The Free Economy and the Strong State*, Macmillan, London, 1988.

open political discussion and lobbying, they should find variety, choice and delegation through market activity alone, and not through further political forms. Choice must be channelled into acceptable paths. This is again logical and coherent, but it does indicate the rather severe limitations imposed on the apparent liberalism or indeed permissiveness of the new right's rallying cry of "freedom of choice".

On a different level, supporters of the present government's frequent assertions of strong central power argue that this is necessary as a temporary phase. The state has to wield power—whether against local government, trade unions, the medical and legal professions, the universities or whatever—until the proper conditions for a society run on market principles have been established, after which the state can adopt a lower profile. Somewhat similarly, Marxists used to talk about how the state would wither away once it had secured the basis of the revolution, and so there was no need to feel uncomfortable at the tendency for Communist governments to concentrate power in very few hands . . .

That answer takes the Government's new right language at face value. It assumes that "Thatcherism" is to be seen, first and foremost, as the embodiment or instrument of a radical neo-liberal project, the over-riding purpose of which is to create the conditions in which market freedom can flourish. The second answer takes a different tack. It focuses on the polity rather than on the economy and on the traditional elements in Thatcherism rather than on the novel ones. In broad outline, it is that—as James Bulpitt suggests—the continuities between the 1980s and previous decades are more striking than the differences; that the fundamental, overriding object of Thatcherism is not to free the market but to restore traditional authority; and that the centralism of the Thatcher governments is to be seen as yet another turn in an old and familiar road. Central government, in this perspective, has acted defensively rather than aggressively. Rather than trying to take ancient powers and competences away from local government, it has tried to return it to the condition of subordination which the British political class has always thought appropriate for it.

European Comparisons

This suggests that it is over-simplified to see recent British developments as the simple implementation of a general new-right agenda. Indeed, it seems clear that many of them are peculiar to the British. Recently accumulating evidence suggests that in western Europe and the United States the trends have been exactly the reverse. A recent special issue of the *European Journal of Political Research*[2] showed Britain running

[2] Michael Goldsmith and Kenneth Newton (eds), *Centralisation and Decentralisation: Changing Patterns of Intergovernmental Relations in Advanced Western Societies*, special issue of *European Journal of Political Research*, vol. 16, no. 4, July 1988. See especially

clearly counter-trend, with even such resolute centralisers as the French[3] and Spanish[4] decentralising fast and on the whole genuinely. Governments faced with demands for regional autonomy not dissimilar to those emanating from Scotland and Northern Ireland have tried to respond creatively, not by defiantly banging down the central lid.

Perhaps most telling in the *EJPR* collection was Howard Wolman's contrast[5] between the apparently very similar administrations of Mrs Thatcher and Ronald Reagan. President Reagan pursued with some vigour the familiar strategy of the US right of reinforcing states and local government rights, making no attempt to damage the autonomy of sub-federal institutions.

The authors in the second part of our book address some of these comparisons, concentrating on the European experience. Douglas Ashford, an American scholar, finds that recent (and not so recent) history reverses the old contrast between centralist France and decentralist Britain. John Stewart and Gerry Stoker examine some imaginative attempts to respond to calls for more local government autonomy in Scandinavia. It is notable that these similar policies have been pursued by governments of various political colour: Social Democratic in Sweden, mainly neo-liberal in Denmark, both of these in Norway and broad coalitions in Finland.

One aspect of all this is sufficiently important to rate as a major surprise. The UK is now alone among the larger nation states in resolutely denying any semblance of *regional* political expression, and the smaller European states are in any case already only the size of regions. There are now strong indications that this may be one of the factors behind the country's continuing *economic* as much as democratic weaknesses. An Americo-German team of researchers has recently drawn attention to the role of regional economic decision-making by the state governments of Massachusetts and Baden-Württemberg[6]— controlled respectively by US Democrats and German Christian Democrats. Within this volume Josef Esser also considers the latter but adds to it Social–Democratic Nordrhein–Westfalen and a brief SPD–Green experiment in Hessen; and Linda Weiss considers the economic activities of both Communist and Christian–Democratic regional governments in Italy.

Is there perhaps something about population units of around three to

L. J. Sharpe, "The growth and decentralisation of the modern democratic state", pp. 365–380.

[3] Edmond Preteceille, "Decentralisation in France: new citizenship or restructuring hegemony?", in *ibid.*, pp. 409–424.

[4] Josep Valles and Montserrat Foix, "Decentralisation in Spain: a review", in *ibid.*, pp. 395–407.

[5] Howard Wolman, "Understanding recent trends in central-local relations: centralisation in Great Britain and decentralisation in the United States", in *ibid.*, pp. 425–435.

[6] Charles Sabel *et al.*, *Regional Prosperities Compared: Massachusetts and Baden-Württemberg in the 1980s*, Wissenschaftszentrum Berlin, 1987.

FOREWORD

eight million (the size of many US states, regions of the larger European states, or the small European nation states themselves) that makes policy-making between public authorities and business organisations particularly useful and flexible? Is Britain missing something by having no autonomous political institutions at this level?

Consideration of such issues, which cannot be resolved within this volume, takes us some way from our starting point of why the Thatcher government has had such difficulties with local government. It also takes us, as the variety of political parties making use of decentralisation in various countries shows, from simple discussions of left and right or old and new right. It leaves us reflecting on certain peculiarities in the way the British have chosen to organise their political life—peculiarities that often turn out to be very different from the contrasts that the British have usually assumed exist between themselves and various "foreigners". And it leaves us wondering whether these peculiarities always work to our advantage.

****

Since its foundation in 1930, *The Political Quarterly* has tried to explore issues of emerging public importance in both Britain and elsewhere, mainly but by no means exclusively from a left-of-centre point of view. It does this primarily through its regular quarterly pages, but also through occasional conferences and seminars or, as in the present case, through a book devoted to a question of particular topicality and importance.

CC
DM
The Editors,
The Political Quarterly

PART I
THE BRITISH CASE

THE THREAT TO THE AUTONOMY OF ELECTED LOCAL GOVERNMENT

IT IS fashionable to talk of the declining discretion of local government in Britain. Read academic journals, newspapers or the local government press and the obituaries of local power and autonomy are there for all to see. Such a view is hardly surprising given that the present Government has apparently devoted itself to regular and progressively more extensive legislation against local authorities.

A description of this legislation would now cover several pages. The intention of the new laws and the rhetoric of ministers have clearly suggested that the high spending and restrictive practices of local authorities were the main reasons for action. Any decline in local autonomy will have been an accidental by-product of attempts to lower spending and manpower, to cap rates, to abolish unnecessary tiers of local government and to protect ratepayers. More recently, the Government has stated that it wishes to strengthen local accountability and to break local authorities' monopolies as suppliers of public services.

But, has such a decline in autonomy actually taken place? The fact that local authorities' overall revenue expenditure is at its highest ever level in real terms, and that manpower has recently drifted upwards following a marginal fall in the early 1980s, suggests that all the present Government's efforts to reduce the size of local government have, despite increasing intervention, failed to deliver the desired control. The political will of members coupled with the skill of senior officers has ensured that, somehow, spending continued to evade control. In the words of a chief officer at the now defunct Greater London Council, the result of the recent power-battle between central and local government has been a "dishonourable draw".

If one of the Government's chief policies has been to reduce local authorities' revenue spending, and yet no such cut has taken place, it is at least arguable that no significant reduction in autonomy has taken place. Local government has been free to decide to exceed central expenditure plans. In fact, as will be argued later, some reductions in

* Tony Travers is Director of Research of The Greater London Group at the London School of Economics. He is adviser to the Education, Science and Arts Select Committee of the House of Commons. Last year he published *The Politics of Local Government Finance*, and recently he co-authored *The London Government Handbook*.

autonomy have occurred, though not yet to the point where local authorities' freedom has been badly impaired. However, an environment has been created in which the move to reductions in real autonomy will be easy to make.

Background

Changes in the scope and autonomy of local government have taken place at intervals throughout the twentieth century. It is clearly possible for the scope of local government to change, i.e. by the removal or addition of a service, without necessarily affecting autonomy. Equally, autonomy could be increased or reduced independently of the range of services provided by local government. The scope of British local government has been decreased, for example with the transfer of national assistance, water and gas to central government or its agencies. In the last thirty years the scope of other services such as education and personal social services has been much increased. Recent legislation is likely to reduce the scope of local government in the early 1990s.

Autonomy was reduced in the early part of the century as local authorities found themselves increasingly given nationally-imposed duties to provide services. In effect, the freedom to decide not to provide services was removed. Often, this involved the government attempting to ensure that a service which had been developed in some parts of the country was extended to all authorities. The system of percentage grants which developed from the latter part of the nineteenth century onwards meant that much of the grant which was paid out of national taxation in support of local services was only paid provided that the expenditure fulfilled conditions laid down by central government. But, within general duties, authorities were often given considerable discretion to determine levels of provision.

With the replacement of specific, percentage grants by a general grant in 1958, a major step was taken towards greater autonomy for local authorities. Although the percentage grants had not generally been used to determine the detail of local government spending, they involved validation by central departments of what individual authorities spent money on. After 1958 the bulk of grant support to local authorities was by the way of a general grant. That is, payment of grant was not tied to use on any particular service.

The move to a general grant in 1958 was followed by a period during which local government expenditure was expanded. During the 1960s and early 1970s, successive governments encouraged local authorities to improve education and other social services provision. The level of grant support to local government was increased, so as to take pressure off ratepayers during a period when the scope of the existing services provided by local authorities increased. According to the Green Paper 'Paying for Local Government' (Cmnd 9714), local authority current expenditure and manpower increased annually on average by 3.75 and 3.5 per cent respectively during the 1960s. During the 1970s, current expenditure increased by 3 per cent annually; on average, though, much of the growth was concentrated in the earlier years of the decade. Capital expenditure also increased in the 1960s and early 1970s.

The fact that local government was at this time financed out of a locally-raised tax and a largely general grant gave local authorities relative freedom in the way they used their resources at a time when their total resources expanded in response to government encouragement. Apart from the removal of water and some remaining health services from local authorities in 1974, the local government service base was broadly unaltered. Extra resources allowed the bulk of local authority provision to expand rapidly. Central government retained influence over some of the detail of this provision, for example the deployment of teachers and general provision of the police. Overall, however, the period from 1958 to 1975 was one in which local authorities enjoyed relative autonomy.

The Period from 1975 to 1979

It is against this background of changes in the scope and autonomy of local government in England and Wales that more recent developments must be judged. The period from 1975 to 1988 has been significantly different from the years between 1958 and 1975. There has been a move back towards the use of specific, percentage grants, as well as a trend towards more direct central involvement in local government decision-making. This trend became established between 1975 and 1979.

The Western economies were enormously affected by the oil price rises of 1973 and 1974. Britain was also afflicted by industrial turmoil and inflation of over 20 per cent. Local government structure was reorganised in 1974 (1975 in Scotland) in a period when the domestic economic and political system was under immense pressure. Rate rises averaged 30 per cent in 1974–75, which was exceptionally high by the standards prevailing at the time. In response to what was seen as a "crisis" in local authority finance (the evidence for such a crisis being, among other things, the high interest rate rises), the Government set up the Layfield Committee in 1974 to inquire into the whole of local government finance in Britain.

General economic difficulties led the Government to seek assistance from the International Monetary Fund in 1976. Conditions imposed by the IMF—in exchange for a loan—included the reduction of public expenditure. The revision downwards of public expenditure plans included lower current and capital spending for local government. To emphasise the need for restraint, the level of central government grant support was cut back from its all time high level of 66.5 per cent, reached in 1975–76.

5

Crisis in the finances of central and local government at this time appears to have coincided with—or may have been triggered by—a change in public attitude towards the public sector. Higher expenditure in local authorities in the 1950s, 1960s and early 1970s, had been accompanied by the view that services such as education, housing and social services could lead to improvements in general social conditions. By the mid-1970s it was becoming clear that no sudden, major change had taken place. Provision was higher, but output appeared little altered. This gap between 1960s' expectations and 1970s' achievement is important in understanding changes in attitude towards local government autonomy which started under Labour in 1975–76.

Attempts to reduce local authority current and capital expenditure in the period 1975 to 1977 were relatively successful. Between 1975–76 and 1977–78 current expenditure by local government in the UK fell by 1.1 per cent, while capital spending was down by 33 per cent. Aggregate exchequer grant to local authorities fell from 66.5 per cent of relevant expenditure in 1975–76 to 61 per cent (at the time of the RSG settlement) in 1979–80. The fact that local government expenditure had stopped rising meant that it was far less easy to finance increases in expenditure on desirable items. Moreover, there was a greater chance that there would be disagreements between central departments and local authorities about where changes in spending should occur. As a result, pressure started to grow within the Government to increase the use of specific grants once again. The Department of Education and Science was keen to introduce a specific grant for in-service teacher-training, while a White Paper on "Policy for the Inner Cities" (Cmnd 6845) advocated the use of additional specific grants. The table below shows changes in the Rate Support Grant percentage and in specific grants as a percentage of aggregate exchequer grant between 1975–76 and 1979–80. Thus, as pressure intensified on local authorities because of reductions in general grant, the level of specific grant within overall grant began to increase. Specific grants offered central departments the possibility of influencing local government without the need to take direct control over services. The increased desire on the part of the centre to encourage authorities as a whole to behave in particular ways was also made clear by other policy initiatives.

TABLE 1 RSG PERCENTAGE AND SPECIFIC GRANTS 1975–6 TO 1979–80
(OUT-TURN) (ENGLAND AND WALES)

	1975–76	1976–77	1977–78	1978–79	1979–80
RSG %	66.4	65.0	62.2	61.2	59.6
Specific grants as % of exchequer grant	12.9	13.7	14.3	14.6	16.3

Source: Tony Travers, *The Politics of Local Government Finance*, George Allen & Unwin, pp. 213–4.

THE THREAT TO AUTONOMY

A Green Paper ("Local Government Finance") published in 1977, outlined a new "unitary grant" which was designed to replace the existing needs and resources elements of the Rate Support Grant. In fact, unitary grant had first emerged in the Department of the Environment's evidence to the Layfield Committee. Unitary grant would not only replace the major part of the existing RSG, but would also allow the government to taper off grant from authorities which chose to spend above levels considered acceptable by central government. The committee accepted that such a grant would be an appropriate part of a system of local government finance with greater central government control. The Green Paper was concerned with accountability: "provided the assessment of an authorities' spending need is accurate, ratepayers would be in a position to ask if the rate poundage were above the standard rate poundage, whether their local authority was less efficient or was providing services to a higher level than other, similar authorities . . .". Local authorities opposed unitary grant on the grounds that it would give central government immense potential power to penalise high spending. The Labour Government which proposed unitary grant had no parliamentary majority. Thus, the move to what the Layfield Committee accepted would be an appropriate grant for a system of local government with more central control was resisted. No changes to local government finance took place in the wake of the 1977 Green Paper. Nevertheless, the Government's desire to introduce a grant which would have offered scope for greater influence over local authority expenditure had been made clear.

Further evidence of a central department's desire to encourage particular behaviour by particular authorities was given by the Department of Transport's use of Transport Supplementary Grant (TSG). In the latter years of the 1974–1979 Labour administration, Transport Secretary William Rodgers cut TSG to both Oxfordshire and South Yorkshire. In the former authority this reduction was a response to the county council's failure to provide "adequate" (in the Secretary of State's view) subsidies for public transport. In South Yorkshire, the reduction in TSG was a response to *excessive* transport subsidy.

Besides these efforts to use financial mechanisms to influence local government, and thus to curtail its autonomy, Prime Minister James Callaghan voiced concern about the quality of local government's major service. At Oxford in 1976 Callaghan spoke at Ruskin College on education standards, making it clear that the existing service was failing to provide education of a kind appropriate for the nation's requirements. A Green Paper (Cmnd 6869) summarised the Prime Minister's case: "the school system is geared to promote the importance of academic learning and careers with the result that pupils, especially the more able, are prejudiced against work in the productive industry and trade; that teachers lack experience, knowledge and understanding of trade and industry; that curricula are not related to the realities of

7

most pupils' work after leaving school; and that pupils leave school with little or no understanding of the workings, or the importance, of the wealth-producing sector of our economy". Given that education was local government's largest service, the Government's criticism was fairly explicit accusation that local authorities were failing.

By the end of the 1970s, public sector housing had also become criticised. A 1977 Green paper entitled "Housing Policy: A consultative document" (Cmnd 6851) spelled out the Government's concern about the state of housing, and by implication, local authority involvement in the service: ". . . despite a sharp rise in total housing expenditure in recent years, problems persist. Housing is sometimes discussed as though little had been achieved and things are getting worse . . . some areas have been left behind by the general improvement in housing standards, especially in the inner cities, where there are concentrations of run down housing and the problems are compounded by other social and economic difficulties . . .".

So, in addition to reducing the growth in expenditure and seeking to influence local government's decision-making power, the Government had openly questioned the quality of major council services. By the 1979 General Election, the stage was set for Mrs Thatcher's Government's more sustained efforts to reform local government and, eventually, to reduce its autonomy.

The Conservatives and Local Government 1979–1987

The Thatcher Government's approach to local government was implicit in the 1979 Conservative election manifesto and campaign. Public expenditure was to be cut back. On the other hand, defence spending was to increase in real-terms, while health and social security were to have their real terms spending maintained. Since defence, health and social security are controlled by central government, it was inevitable that if public expenditure was to be cut overall the bulk of any reduction would have to be concentrated outside central government's major expenditure programme. Local government and the nationalised industries made up those parts of public expenditure outside central government's direct control.

Thus, it was implicit in the Conservatives' 1979 platform that local government expenditure would have to be reduced. Immediately after taking office in July 1979, the new Environment Secretary announced lower public expenditure plans for local authorities for 1979–80. In addition, it was announced that the Rate Support Grant for 1979–80 was to be cut back by £300m so as to encourage authorities to reduce spending. At this time reducing the overall level of RSG was the main weapon available to central government if it wished to influence local authority expenditure. In the 1960s and early 1970s, rising grant levels had been used to encourage higher council spending. By the late 1970s, cuts in RSG were being used in the attempt to discourage spending.

The lack of direct control over local authority expenditure was stressed by Environment Secretary Michael Heseltine in a statement to the Consultative Council on Local Government Finance on July 31, 1979: "within the overall need for spending reductions, the Government thinks it right to give local authorities the maximum freedom to decide on the allocation of funds in accordance with their own spending priorities". Despite Mr Heseltine's assurances, he made a further announcement in September 1979 which pointed the way to more direct attempts to influence (if not directly to control) individual authorities. Speaking to a joint conference of the three local authority associations, he said that no government, of whatever party, would or could tolerate a situation where local authorities pursued their own ends regardless of the expressed views of the government.

Despite this concern with local authorities' (by implication, individual councils') spending, the Secretary of State could only seek to influence local authorities by making overall cuts in the level of grant. It was not possible, under the then existing system of Rate Support Grant, to make selective cuts in authorities' grant. There existed no power to restrict the rates or expenditure of individual authorities, merely the possibility of overall grant reductions and of exhortation by the Secretary of State.

The Local Government, Planning and Land Act, 1980 marked a significant step to increasing central influence over individual authorities. The Act introduced a new "block grant" to replace the "needs" and "resources" elements of the Rate Support Grant. More importantly, the new grant system allowed the Government to taper off grant from any authority which chose to spend over a standard level of expenditure. This measure of standard expenditure, which came to be known as Grant Related Expenditure (GRE), was set up by central government after consultation with local authorities. This block grant was, in fact, simply the re-named "unitary" grant which Labour had proposed in their 1977 Green Paper. The Department of the Environment, which had first proposed such a grant to the Layfield Committee, had now found an Environment Secretary who was prepared to give them more detailed pressure on individual local authorities.

Block grant was widely seen as a significant, constitutional step. Local government autonomy would inevitably be challenged by a grant system which effectively tapered off or reduced support as spending increased. This challenge was ensured by the fact that central government determined the rate of grant change as spending increased. Also, a central government set the figure which each authority in the country "needed" to spend—the GRE. Inevitably this figure was seen as a government-approved norm. In accepting the idea of such a norm, the Government was making a move which previous governments had largely resisted, that is, taking action to influence individual councils.

9

Discussing the transitional arrangements which the Government proposed to bridge the year between the old RSG system and the operation of block grant, junior Environment Minister Lord Bellwin claimed: ". . . . surely it is right for the Government to spotlight those authorities who are not willing to conform to national policy objectives. I am sure that the country at large thinks it right and proper that those authorities who refuse to cooperate should bear the cost. The Government is entitled to expect the cooperation of local authorities whose individual objectives must be subordinate to the national interest". The final sentence quoted is a straightforward appeal for a kind of democratic centralism. Block grant was the first major step towards the shaping of a system of local government finance in which local autonomy would be much curtailed.

Block grant started to operate in 1981–2. During that year, the Government announced that it would superimpose on block grant a system of expenditure targets and grant penalties. These sophistications had the effect of taking block grant away from any authority which exceeded a spending target set up by the Department of the Environment. This refinement to the basic grant system made it even more punitive for authorities which decided to spend above Government spending benchmarks. Local authority powers to set supplementary rates (i.e. more than one rate a year) were also taken away. The introduction of block grant, followed by increasingly punitive targets and penalties, failed to bring revenue expenditure down to overall Government plans. Real current expenditure continued to drift gently upwards.

Capital expenditure control had also been changed by the Local Government, Planning and Land Act. However, the change in control over capital—from limits on borrowing to limits on expenditure—had little effect on local autonomy. Capital expenditure had been, and continued to be, broadly controlled by central government. Authorities enjoyed some autonomy over the precise nature of their capital expenditure, though no power to exceed overall allocations. This failure to restrict revenue expenditure was remarkable given the extent to which many authorities lost grant for "overspending". Councillors were prepared to raise rates rather than reduce spending.

During this same period, 1981–82 to 1983–84, the Conservative Government had also sought to find an alternative to domestic rates. Pressure to abolish the rates had emerged within Tory ranks ever since Mrs Thatcher (then Opposition Environment Spokesman) had promised to abolish domestic rates during the October 1974 Election. The clear message of a Green Paper entitled "Alternatives to Domestic Rates" (Cmnd 8449, 1981) was that there was no realistic alternative to rates.

Out of these failures to bring down local government revenue spending and to find an acceptable alternative to domestic rates, came a major proposal: rate limitation. The 1983 Conservative manifesto promised that the Government would take powers to cap the rates of high spending councils, while the metropolitan counties and Greater London Council which, it was argued, were wasteful, would be abolished.

Rate limitation was duly introduced. Environment Secretary Patrick Jenkin accepted that capping the rates of authorities was a matter of constitutional importance. Local authorities had been free to set whatever rates they chose since the sixteenth century. During the second reading Mr Jenkin defended the new central powers thus: "We have a duty to protect ratepayers from blatant exploitation. We have a duty to ensure that all parts of the public sector work within national economic policies. Other efforts to make these few authorities see reason have failed . . .". Other Conservatives were extremely suspicious of the proposed loss of local autonomy and were not convinced that local accountability was defective. Mr Geoffrey (now Lord) Rippon, who had been Environment Secretary in the 1970s, claimed that the Bill introducing capping was "one of the most deplorable Bills that has been brought before the House in all the time that I have been a Minister . . . its nature is undemocratic and contrary to the spirit of our unwritten constitution . . .". Other leading Conservatives were even less charitable.

The Government's large majority ensured that rate limitation became law and that the GLC and metropolitan counties were abolished. Rates were limited (in 18 authorities) for the first time in 1985–86. Another significant step had been taken towards reducing local autonomy. A majority of high-spending—and generally large—authorities were now in the position that they could only raise their rates up to a level set by central government. Many authorities had to cut their rates.

The metropolitan counties and the GLC, which were significant, county-wide local authorities in the major city areas were abolished and their services passed to lower tier authorities, to appointed and nominated boards and to the Government. In the sense that some powers passed away from elected local government and that significant concentrations of local power were removed, abolition reduced local autonomy and the capacity of individual authorities to act as a buffer against central departments.

During Mrs Thatcher's second administration, central departments started to search in earnest for ways of directing local authorities to spend in particular ways or to avoid using local government altogether. Ten years of slow or zero growth since 1975 had meant little money was available for new initiatives. Central government at this time was awash with bright ideas about how education, training, urban sprawl and other problems should be tackled. In the short term the Government turned to increased use of specific grants and to the development of agencies which could by-pass local government.

In education and training there was a significant movement towards specific grants and central agencies. The Manpower Services Commission (subsequently renamed the Training Commission, though now abolished altogether) developed a range of training schemes. In 1985–86 vocational non-advanced further education was transferred from local authority control to MSC funding. MSC allocated specific grants to local authorities to finance a Technical and Vocational Education Initiative.

A range of specific grants was also introduced by the Department of Education and Science. Although the DES's specific grants were constrained to the support of no more than one per cent of education expenditure, the development of Education Support Grant and of a grant for in-service teacher training marked an important shift within central government. DES had been lobbying for a specific grant for in-service training since the mid-1970s. DES wanted to be able to pump-prime expenditure within local authorities. Education Support Grants have been given to authorities for such items as combating drug abuse, information technology, and science education. Authorities only receive ESGs if they use the grant for the specific purpose intended. DES priorities could be pursued.

DES went even further in 1986 by announcing that new, centrally-funded schools were to be set up. They were to be called City Technology Colleges, and would be independent foundations. Capital costs would be met in part by the private sector, though long-term revenue support would come from DES. CTCs were intended to cater for inner-city pupils who could pursue an education with a technical focus. CTCs were a further attempt—as was MSC funding of technical and vocational training—to by-pass local government. As pupils pass from local authority schools to CTCs, autonomy will be further reduced.

In 1987 the Government took control over teachers' pay and conditions. Even though local authorities remain employers and can, to a certain extent, determine numbers, the government now determines pay and conditions for teachers. As teachers' salaries make up a major element of local government spending, this transfer of power was significant and symbolic in reducing local government autonomy.

Urban development was an activity where successive governments had by-passed local authorities. In the 1970s, small specific grants were paid out to local authorities with urban problems. Grants were stepped up following the Labour Government's Green Paper "Policy for the Inner Cities" (Cmnd 6845). Partnerships were created bringing together central and local government, plus other bodies, to devise strategies for inner-city areas with the most problems Funding rose steeply, though never by enough to deal with the vast difficulties of these inner areas.

The Conservative Government since 1979 adopted new policies which had by-passed local authorities and removed their powers. Emphasis switched from social to economic policies. Enterprise Zones were created by the Local Government, Planning and Land Act, giving companies within a zone a number of concessions, including exemption

12

from rates. By reducing financial and physical controls in an area, it was felt that enterprise could flourish.

Urban Development Corporations were also used to make rapid changes in inner cities. Building on the idea of new town development corporations, the 1980 Act gave the Environment Secretary powers to declare urban development corporations. In the early 1980s, UDCs were announced for London Docklands and Merseyside. The Corporations were vested with publicly-held land and considerable resources, and were given powers over planning and transport. Because UDCs were made up of members appointed by the Government, they were able to act in the way the Government itself wished and without the need for local democratic participation. Task Force and City Action Teams composed of civil servants and those from industry were also set up to co-ordinate regeneration proposals in various inner city areas. Local authorities had limited inputs to these new bodies, which were primarily concerned with involving and encouraging private sector developers.

During 1988 the Government announced a new City Grant to replace urban development and regeneration grants. The purpose of this new grant was to pay money directly to the private sector, with no local authority involvement. Thus, it is now possible for the Government to develop assistance for inner-city areas without using local government at all. City Grants, UDCs and Enterprise Zones effectively by-pass local authorities, while UDCs reduce local autonomy.

Another example of reduced local autonomy occurred in transport. In 1984, the Government took powers to transfer London Transport from control by the Secretary of State for Transport. In effect, LT became a nationalised industry under the general control of central government.

An Analysis of the 1979–1987 Developments

Block grant was introduced to give the Government more direct power to influence individual authorities' expenditure. The power to raise a supplementary rate was moved in 1982, while the Rate Act, 1984, allowed the Government to limit individual authorities' rates for the first time ever. GLC and metropolitan county abolition had the effect of removing a powerful buffer between district councils and the Government, while also transferring some powers out of local government.

The continuing attempts to restrain local authority expenditure activity—which started in the mid-1970s—were coupled with an increasing use of specific grants within a falling total of grant. Table 2 shows changes in the level of RSG and specific grants as a proportion of aggregate grant between 1979–80 and 1987–88. As in the earlier table which showed the same information between 1975–76 and 1979–80, specific grants have grown in importance while overall grant has declined.

TABLE 2 RSG PERCENTAGE AND SPECIFIC GRANTS (OUT-TURN), 1979–80
TO 1987–88 (ENGLAND AND WALES)

	1979–80	1980–1	1981–2	1982–3	1983–4	1984–5	1985–6	1986–7	1987–8
RSG %	59.6	59.0	55.8	52.7	50.8	50.9	47.7	45.8	46.3
Specific grants as % of exchequer grant	16.3	16.3	17.4	19.3	20.6	23.1	22.5	23.7	24.8

This move towards specific, percentage grants was accompanied by use of specific grants by the Manpower Services Commission and by the wholesale transfer of a part of further education to MSC control. Taken with other transfers (primarily teachers' salaries) and the by-passing of local authorities for inner city regeneration, the period from 1979–87 appears as one of unparalleled reduction in local autonomy.

But, as stated at the start of this paper, the effect on local government overall has not been such as to suggest an overwhelming transfer of power and a major reduction of autonomy. Local authority revenue spending stands at its highest-ever real level. Manpower is barely changed since the late 1970s. The core of local government provision remains unaltered, except for a few minor transfers. There are more and bigger specific, percentage grants, but they still make up only about a quarter of RSG and about 10 per cent of revenue income. Local government had managed to preserve a remarkable part of its autonomy despite central government's clear desire to transfer power and influence to itself.

This ability to preserve a considerable level of autonomy despite the effects of a powerful central government eager to curtail local power must have derived, at least in part, from the traditional freedom of British local authorities to set their own spending and taxation levels. Although this freedom was never enshrined in a written constitution, the strength of tradition within British constitutional arrangements was a hurdle which the Government has found it difficult to overcome in reducing local autonomy. On countless occasions while the block grant, rate limitation and abolition legislation were being passed, the Opposition and Government backbenchers accused the Government of behaving in an unconstitutional way. Ministers responded by reference to the Government's electoral mandate. Nevertheless, at no point did the Government attempt—as it might have done—to take direct control over the spending decisions of individual councils.

Another constraint on the Government was the scope and complexity of local government provision. Ministers clearly did not feel able either to stop providing any of local government's services, nor were they prepared to transfer the bulk of such services to central departments. Proposals were made on a number of occasions during the 1980s to privatise parts of services such as refuse collection and leisure facilities.

14

THE THREAT TO AUTONOMY

The transfer of education to more direct central control was also promoted (often within the Conservative Party) from time to time. The risks involved in transferring—or removing—significant public services from local authorities were too great for the Government. However, immediately before and following the 1987 General Election, the Government started to evolve new policies for local government which potentially threaten the traditional autonomy of local authorities. These policies involve replacing the domestic rates with a flat-rate "community charge" (or poll tax); allowing tenants to opt out of local authority control; allowing schools far greater autonomy, and putting many more government services out to competitive tender. These policies were to be pursued as part of a new approach to local government, enhancing the operation of the market and allowing individuals more choice in the provision of public services.

The Future for Local Government

Four major pieces of local government legislation passed through Parliament during the 1987–88 session. Between them they could radically alter the scope of what local authorities provide and the way in which many services are provided and financed. While each piece of legislation evolved separately from the others, there can be little doubt that their philosophical origins were similar, deriving from the ideas of right-wing think tanks and policy units. Earlier criticisms of local provision, voiced by the previous Labour Government and in Mrs Thatcher's first two administrations, clearly made it easier for these new policies to capture the imagination of senior politicians. The broad purpose of these new policies was to break down the traditional local authority, to force it to employ fewer staff directly and to make it compete more widely in the provision of public services. The introduction of a "community charge" (as the poll tax was called) was intended by Ministers to strengthen the idea of charging for a basket of specific services which local government provides.

The Local Government Act, 1988 was primarily designed to compel all local authorities to put out the provision of many basic services to competitive tender. As such, it built on earlier legislation which compelled local authority direct labour building organisations to compete for contracts with private contractors. A similar contracting-out exercise had also taken place in the National Health Service. Local authority workforces would have to compete with private contractors to provide services such as refuse collection, building maintenance and cleansing. Most manual services will be brought within the scope of competitive tendering in the period after August 1989, though the Government has also taken powers to extend competitive tendering at a later date to administrative and other parts of local government such as architects and computing departments.

15

The Local Government Finance Act will replace domestic rates with a community charge or poll tax, to be paid—with very few exceptions and modifications—by all adults. Non-domestic rates will in future be an assigned revenue, set by central government, collected centrally and redistributed to authorities on the basis of their adult population. The Rate Support Grant will be reaffirmed in a way which is intended to make it simpler, and will in future be called "Revenue Support Grant" (RSG). Because the Government will be responsible for the allocation of RSG and the non-domestic rates, which together make up about three-quarters of local government revenue income, only one quarter of councils' income (the poll tax) will be in the control of local government. This position compares with the present system in which about 55 per cent of income is derived from the locally-set rates. In Wales, the proportion to be met out of poll tax will be even lower than in England, though the existing rate-borne proportion is also lower.

The new system of local government finance will work in such a way that all expenditure above centrally-determined measurement of spending need will fall on community charge. The needs assessment for each authority will therefore be crucial in determining the level of grant, and non-domestic rates will also affect authorities' charges. Changes in an authority's expenditure will be only one of a number of influences on the local tax.

The fact that a high proportion of authorities' revenue income will be made up from central sources will affect local authorities in two ways. First, authorities will find that their level of local tax is often influenced by changes in their income from central government. Secondly, politicians and officials may start to take account of the fact that three-quarters of local authority income is centrally-determined, arguing that as the bulk of local government income is derived from the government, then the bulk of decisions about local services should be made centrally. The Act also allows the government to limit the community charge (and thus the spending) of any authority spending over £15m.

The Education Reform Act will affect all aspects of publicly-financed education. As far as local government is concerned, the most important change will take place in schools. In future, the finance and management of almost all schools (and further education colleges) will pass from local authorities to control by governors. Only a small proportion (about 10 per cent) of expenditure on schools will remain in direct control of local government, though councils will have overall responsibility to ensure that schools fill their legal duties.

Schools will also be given the possibility of opting out of local government. Following a vote by governors and/or parents, a school will be able to apply to the Secretary of State for Education to opt out of local authority control. If the Secretary of State agrees with the proposal to opt out, the school would be maintained directly by the Department of Education and Science. All assets would transfer from the local authority concerned to the school, though the DES would recharge the costs of running the school to the authority. The local authority would then have no responsibility for the opted-out institution.

While it is certain that all but the smallest schools and colleges will have financial and administrative control devolved to them, it is less easy to predict how far schools will opt out of local government. Some institutions will inevitably apply to opt out, for example, if they are threatened with closure or if they disagree fundamentally with their local authority over policy. The extent to which the majority of schools decide to apply to opt out will depend upon the success of administrative devolution and on the relative financial advantages of opting out or staying within local government. Mrs Thatcher was widely quoted during 1987 as saying that she hoped that "a majority" of schools would opt out of local government. It is possible that the Prime Minister's personal commitment to the removal of schools from local government may yet be important in determining how many schools leave their controlling authorities. The more schools leave local government, the greater is the reduction in the scope and autonomy of local authorities.

The Education Reform Act will also introduce a "national curriculum", which will mean that for the first time in England and Wales the Government will be responsible for what is taught in schools. Up till now this responsibility rested, in a general sense, with local authorities, though individual schools and teachers tended to make most decisions about the curriculum.

Another important change introduced by the new education legislation will be the removal of the polytechnics and other major colleges from local government. A new Polytechnics and Colleges Funding Council (PCFC) will take over the financing of this sector. £800m will thus be transferred from local government to the new, centrally-appointed PCFC. Almost half of further education will be moved from local to central control. About a quarter of non-advanced further education had been transferred from local authority to Manpower Services Commission control in 1985–6.

The fourth major piece of legislation was the Housing Act. Like the Education Reform Act, this new law allowed people to opt out of local authority control. Tenants of council houses and flats were offered the possibility of leaving the control and administration of local authorities and opting instead for control by housing associations, approved private landlords or cooperatives. As with opting out in education, it is not possible to predict how many tenants will take advantage of their right to opt out. Again, financial incentives will be important in determining how many individuals make a change. Some authorities will actively encourage tenants to opt out, while others will oppose such transfers.

In addition to initiating opting out, the Housing Act set up Housing Action Trusts (HATs). These new bodies will be similar to urban development corporations, in that they will be centrally appointed and funded and will be wound up after a fixed period. The purpose of HATs will be to take over estates or blocks of poor local authority housing stock and to improve it. Once the improvement has been completed, the housing will be passed to housing associations, approved private landlords, cooperatives or, possibly, to local authorities.

Opting out and HATs could lead to a major reduction in local government involvement in social housing. The Government has made it clear that they hope that in future local government will "enable" social housing rather than providing it directly. That is, the Government sees local authorities as assisting the private and voluntary sectors of housing, plus maintaining its own residential stock, though with little or no addition to existing housing. Further legislation will follow in 1988–89 to stop local authorities subsidising council house rents out of local taxation.

Taken together, the Local Government, Local Government Finance, Education Reform and Housing Acts suggest that the Government has moved to a new phase in its relationship with local government. Having attempted to reduce and redirect spending between 1976 and 1987, attention has now turned to making local authorities compete in the provision of services while also allowing individuals and groups to transfer parts of services out of local government and into smaller units of provision.

Transfers made possible by the new education and housing legislation involve moves of power in two directions. Although schools and tenants can opt out of local government into control either by governing bodies or by, say, a housing association, the final responsibility for the new institutions will rest with central government. All the local government legislation passed in 1987–88 includes enormous numbers of reserve and appeal powers for central government. Opted out schools and many new semi-private landlords will, in the last resort, be accountable to the relevant Secretary of State.

If a majority of schools and council housing opted out of local government, billions of pounds worth of expenditure would be moved out of local authority control. The fact that the local tax base is a flat-rate poll tax will make it more difficult for authorities to raise additional resources for those services which remain. Because the new rates will, compared with domestic rates, fall more heavily on people with relatively smaller incomes, raising additional resources will inevitably be more difficult than at present. As only a quarter of revenue income will be derived from this community charge, changes in the centrally-determined proportion of local income will give the Government an immense potential influence over the level of local taxation, and thus spending. Competition will become a more important feature of local government's environment. There will be competition to provide individual services, and competition between local authority schools/housing and those in the voluntary and private sectors.

THE THREAT TO AUTONOMY

There can be little doubt that local government scope and autonomy will shrink, while the direct and indirect control by central government departments will increase. Some power will pass to governing bodies, housing associations and other small institutions, thus creating a new kind of local government. Such new institutions will not be elected in the way existing local authorities are, but will generally be appointed (in many cases appointed with the approval of the Government). Final responsibility for many schools, houses and other provisions will be given to Secretaries of State.

Analysis

Although autonomy has not been wholly removed from local authorities in Britain, there has been a trend in recent years to transfer some smaller services from local to central government control; to increase the use of specific grants and generally to seek to influence the expenditure and taxation of individual councils. It is certain that further transfers of control will take place in the years from 1989.

The period since the mid-1970s during which pressure has built up for greater control over local government has coincided with immense social and economic changes in Britain. The extent to which the social and economic changes have influenced the desire to reduce local autonomy is difficult to estimate. There can be little doubt that economic difficulties between 1974 and 1982 led to pressures to cut public expenditure and to critical examination of the activities of government. Central government has consistently found it easier to point to the inadequacies of local authorities and to demand greater spending reductions from local government services than to criticise or rationalise its own activities. Public expenditure plans during the 1980s for local authorities have consistently been less generous than those for central government. Ministers have devoted vast amounts of time to criticising local government and attempting to reform it.

Although recent trends to reduce local autonomy started in the mid-1970s the approaches of Labour and Conservative administrations have differed. Indeed, the 1979 Conservative Government approached local government rather differently in the early part of its period of office from the way it has later on. Labour started to make small reductions in local autonomy by "traditional" means such as reducing the level of Rate Support Grant and increasing use of specific grants. In the period from 1979–87, the Conservatives moved to a position where they could have greater influence over individual councils, coupled with far more zealous use of specific grants. Beyond 1987, it is clear that the dominant ideology within the Government, which is to weaken and reform public monopolies, and to break down vested interests, has led to a programme of reforms which are likely to remove parts or all of many services from local authorities and considerably to reduce the autonomy of local government.

During the 1980s, the political divide between central and local government led to pressure on Ministers to reform local authorities in various ways. The Government has prided itself on being right-wing and radical at a time when a number of powerful authorities—particularly in urban areas—have been controlled by radical, left-wing councillors. The lack of shared political objectives between central and local government during the 1980s has contributed to a feeling in central government that it would be easier to achieve social and economic objectives if local authorities were to be made less powerful. Large parliamentary majorities for the Government elected in 1983 and 1987 have ensured that the reform of local government has not been hindered by the Opposition. Although public attitudes (as demonstrated by opinion polling) have generally supported local government and have opposed such reforms as abolition of the GLC and the metropolitan counties and the introduction of rate limitation, the Government has not been irrevocably harmed in national elections by its removal of local autonomy.

Because opinion surveys suggest that matters such as the health service, unemployment and the economy are of predominant interest to electors, it appears that local government—even at times of reform—is not of overwhelming political importance to politicians. Reforms which involve removal of autonomy can be undertaken by the Government without fears for the electoral consequences.

The future for autonomous local government must depend to a large extent on whether the political reaction to education, housing and local government finance reforms in 1989 and beyond is favourable. A reaction against the breaking-down of local government power could create pressure to recreate effective and autonomous local authorities. Alternatively, a change in political fashion might return to favour the concept of powerful local government.

In the short term, however, the autonomy and freedom of local government in Britain looks set to decline. No real thought has yet been given to the kinds of institutional arrangements which will exist in future. Equally, it is not possible to be certain about the impact on the democratic system of the removal of local government power. It is inevitable that individuals will, in future, be more than ever exposed directly to central government and its agencies. The population will have to rely, more than ever before, on Parliament for redress of grievances and to control governmental activity. It is to be hoped that members of Parliament will undertake their increased responsibilities with diligence. If Parliament does not change, the removal of local autonomy will lead to poorer services and a weaker democracy.

CENTRAL CONTROL IN BRITISH URBAN ECONOMIC DEVELOPMENT PROGRAMMES

ALAN HARDING*

SHORTLY after the Conservative triumph in the 1987 General Election, the Prime Minister could be heard placing the economic resurgence of inner city areas, and the restoration of her party's flagging fortunes within them, as top priorities for the third term. Some nine months later the glossy results of deliberations by a specially-convened inner cities Cabinet committee were launched. Shorn of the White Paper status once envisaged for it, "Action for Cities" offered little more than a repackaging of pre-existing inner city initiatives. In one aspect however, the document could be seen as striking. A decade or so earlier a recast Urban Programme, within which economic development was a significant part, had signalled central partnership with, and a full share of policy responsibilities for, local elected councils as crucial to inner area regeneration. Indeed a White Paper had described the local authority as the "natural agency" for delivering public programmes in this field.[1] By 1988, local authorities merited scarcely a single mention in a description of programmes wherein "government" and "business" were to be the dominant influences. Judged in such broad terms, it would not seem to be overstating the case to suggest that we see in this policy area a clear and stark example of the centralist tendencies of successive Thatcher Governments. There would appear to have been a significant shift in policy control from the local to the national elected body. The following looks for the sort of detailed evidence which would be necessary if such a claim were to be validated. First there is a discussion of the utility of the term "centralisation" as it applies to the policy process, and some potential indicators of centralism are suggested. There is then an attempt to assess the extent to which the pre-1979 situation could be regarded as centralist. The evidence for a recent increase in centralisation is then examined, along with the factors which might have brought it about. A concluding section then asks whether recent experience is likely to prove particularly significant to the future of public policy-making in this field.

* The author is a Research Associate in the Centre for Urban Studies at the University of Liverpool. He has previously published work on urban policy whilst undertaking research at the London School of Economics and Nuffield College, Oxford.
[1] *Policy for the Inner Cities*, Cmnd 6845, London: HMSO, 1977.

What is Centralisation?

Centralisation is a term often used by political commentators when discussing Conservative government in Britain since 1979. However, if it is to be useful to political science and to elucidate more than it obscures, the term needs to be more tightly defined than is generally the case. To speak of centralisation at all is to offer an implicit picture of the distribution of power and influence as between the central (national) authority and sub-national and/or non-governmental agencies at different points in time. Unless the assumptions on which this picture is based are made explicit, the term centralisation can offer little insight. For this reason it is worth sketching in some key observations, however mundane, on the balance of power in public policy-making in Britain.[2]

Britain is a unitary state wherein sovereignty lies with Parliament and hence effectively, under conditions of comfortable one-party control, with the government of the day. All sub-national units of governments, whether independently elected or not, are essentially either creatures of statute or organisational offshoots of central departments. The centre is free, subject to there being a willingness to accept the political costs, to change the structure and functions of all subordinate agencies at will: it may even choose to abolish them completely. However, the sheer volume of functions undertaken by the modern state and the geographical area over which they are performed mean that some responsibility for formulating and implementing public policy is necessarily delegated to area-based actors. These actors work in a number of different organisational contexts and their relationship with the centre varies considerably. To borrow one classification, sub-national agencies can be described as either *deconcentrated* or *decentralised*.[3]

Deconcentration is organised primarily to suit the centre's administrative convenience in implementation. In some instances this can mean simply that field administrators employed by central departments assume responsibility for implementing standardised and tightly defined central programmes: in others they may acquire a significant degree of discretion. Only in the latter can we speak of a decentralisation of power, although some agencies, for example the regional offices of departments like Transport and Environment, perform both roles. Decentralised agencies appear in three forms. Central departments themselves combine territorial responsibilities with discretion over the

[2] This discussion draws heavily on the work of Rhodes and Dunleavy. See Dunleavy, P. and Rhodes, R. A. W., "Beyond Whitehall" in Drucker, D., Dunleavy, P., Gamble, A. and Peele, G. (eds) *Developments in British Politics* (revised edition) London: Macmillan, 1984; Dunleavy, P. *Urban Political Analysis*, London: Macmillan, 1980; Rhodes, R. A. W., *Beyond Westminster and Whitehall: The Sub-central Government of Britain* London: Unwin Hyman, 1988.

[3] Hogwood, B. and Keating, M. (eds) *Regional Government in England*, Oxford: Clarendon, 1982, Chap. 1.

performance of certain functions. This is the case for the Scottish, Welsh and Northern Ireland Offices. Central government can also establish quasi-governmental agencies (QGAs) which assume responsibility for particular functions on an area basis. Finally local authorities, whilst constrained by the *ultra vires* principle which limits their actions to those which are expressly permitted by statute, are characterised by varying levels of discretion in the performance of their functions.

Control over the statutory process affords central government the power to specify the form and structure of decentralised administrative units and to designate the powers available to them in the performance of delegated functions. Central control over the policy process can also be achieved through other means. Financial controls can be instituted over the level of central support offered to decentralised agencies and the purposes for which it is used, and over local agencies' power to raise finance independently. Administrative procedures can be tightened through the introduction of stricter programme guidelines, through control over key staff appointments and the acquisition and use of physical assets, the use of veto powers over individual projects, and by the selective distribution of information. The centre can also manipulate the process of policy formulation and implementation such that certain non-governmental interest groups are given greater influence over policy decisions than others. Thus, whilst we might argue that direct implementation by central actors is largely unfeasible, all of the above resources can be used to limit the discretion of decentralised agencies, thereby centralising decision-making.

Decentralised agencies can manipulate their own, often similar resources to retain maximum control over policy-making too. Elected agencies can claim a degree of political legitimacy from the local franchise, although central sovereignty will usually prevail where local mandates conflict significantly with central priorities. All local agencies can use any independent finance-raising powers and their control over human, physical and informational resources to resist bids by the centre to gain greater influence over local decisions and will frequently attempt to mobilise the support of local interest groups in the process.

On the basis of the above we can identify a continuum running between high degrees of centralisation at one end and decentralisation at the other. The point at which any one agency or administrative arrangement appears on this continuum may well differ with the function under consideration. At the former end, central or centrally-appointed actors along with their favoured coalition of interest groups will assume responsibility for policy formulation and implementation. Financial, physical and informational resources will be dominated by these actors and both the statutory base for the particular agency or administrative unit and the "rules of the game" will be decided centrally. At the other end we can hypothesise that a locally elected body with maximum statutory discretion and independent finance-raising powers, dominance over the use of human, physical and informational resources, and freedom from central administrative regulation will exhibit the greatest degree of decentralised power.

It should be noted that the degree of decentralisation does not of itself allow us to predict any particular policy consequences. The extent to which decentralised power is used contrary to the desire of central government is dependent on the existence of a conflict of views between central actors and those in the localities. Such conflict is likely to be sharpest where there are strong ideological differences between central and local political élites, although any group of actors charged with defending the interests of a particular territory will occasionally find themselves in conflict with a central authority whose responsibility it is to balance and accommodate territorial demands. The notion of a continuum is useful in that it helps us to judge how centralised are the arrangements for the performance of functions in a particular policy area at any one period in time. Once located on the continuum, we can assess the extent to which further centralisation has been attempted or achieved through the use of the tools outlined above. The following two sections attempt to do this for urban economic development policy initiatives.

The Pre-1979 Legacy

It is only in the last fifteen years or so, largely as a consequence of the economic recessions of the mid-1970s and early 1980s, that conscious attempts have been made by public authorities to tackle the problem of urban economic decline. That is not to deny that decisions made in the public sector cumulatively have not always had a decisive impact on urban economic wellbeing, but to suggest that there has traditionally been little attempt to measure this nor to see cities as significant units for the purpose of development strategies. Whilst local authorities played an important part in the development of industrial infrastructure, particularly the public utilities, in the early part of the century, post-war industrial and employment policies relied, until the late 1970s, on a combination of macro-economic management and instruments like regional industrial grants and New Towns to redistribute and promote economic activity in particular areas. New Town Corporations, as QGAs, and the existence of limited discretion for regional departmental officials in the operation of regional grants were the only decentralist strands in what was a highly centralised programme wherein the principal urban concern was to decant population and jobs from overcrowded cities. The system of local planning instituted after the last war was designed essentially to regulate conflicting demands for development, not to promote them.

When urban problems did force themselves on to central government's agenda, it was for a combination of ostensibly non-economic reasons.

Despite a background which saw the development of economic activity outside the main conurbations and decline in the economies of older urban areas—leading to the flight from the cities of the more skilled and affluent and the ghettoisation of more vulnerable groups—the "inner city problem" was initially interpreted as being social in essence. The discovery of concentrations of poverty in the cities cast doubt on the efficacy of welfare rather than industrial or employment policies and led to a debate on the need for positive, area-based discrimination in the social services. The political sensitivity about increasing Commonwealth immigration into the conurbations and fear of US-style urban unrest finally provided a trigger for central government action and there followed, in the decade after 1967, a series of central initiatives aimed at improving social provision in small target areas. With the exception of the Urban Programme (UP), which invited local authorities to bid annually for central funds to support specific projects, each new urban experiment tended to be *ad hoc*, thinly resourced, and dominated by central appointees to the exclusion of established decentralised agencies.

As a partial consequence of this, and of the growing urgency of local economic problems, urban local authorities during the 1970s increasingly diversified into economic development functions. The policy area grew despite the absence of any significant statutory basis for action in this field. Programmes had to be cobbled together through piecemeal powers, for example in the development and provision of land and buildings and the subsidisation of rents. The statutory mainstay was in fact a general power provided under Section 137 of the Local Government Act 1972 which allows an authority to spend the proceeds of a twopenny rate in the interests of its area or inhabitants: this was by far the most important finance generator. With one or two exceptions, local policy-making was thus simultaneously unconstrained and un-supported by central government. The exceptions were those authorities which successfully sponsored private bills through Parliament increasing their economic development powers in a modest way. A typical authority at this time might improve land and buildings for industrial and commercial purposes, organise promotional events for the area or its business, and offer business advice and assistance. Despite the relatively uncontroversial nature of such packages, the fact that local authorities were potentially in competition for footloose investment could be construed as being inconsistent with central policies on the location of industry.

Whilst this may have been a spur to central policy development, the arguments raised by some of the experimental social policy initiatives in the mid-1970s certainly had a dramatic effect on central government thinking. Both the Community Development Projects (CDPs) and the Inner Area Studies (IAS) teams produced reports which rejected the "social pathology" approach to the inner city, that is the idea that the problem lay with inner city residents and was soluble through welfare programmes, and argued that a lack of economic opportunity should be the central issue. In 1976, the Environment Secretary announced a scheme to regenerate the run-down East End of Glasgow in a major policy reversal which saw plans for a New Town on the outskirts of the city abandoned. Much of the New Town team was transferred to the Scottish Development Agency (SDA), established in 1975 with a general job-creation remit and powers to provide environmental works, industrial infrastructure and investment, thus providing the Agency with its first experience of specifically urban projects. The somewhat reluctant SDA was charged with co-ordinating administrative machinery which encompassed the city and regional elected authorities, the health authority and the Scottish Special Housing Association as well as local voluntary bodies. The Glasgow Eastern Area Renewal (GEAR) project operated to a wide remit which included economic, environmental and social renewal objectives and programmes. Specific central grant funding was channelled to the scheme via the Scottish Office.

By 1977, with the publication of the inner cities White Paper at a time when the openly racist National Front party was making electoral capital out of the issue of non-white settlement in certain inner city areas, the economic regeneration of inner cities and the abandonment of policies which actively dispersed jobs from these areas had become part of a new orthodoxy. It was also accepted that local agencies had a crucial role to play in the development of new public programmes to tackle economic decline. The White Paper was followed by the Inner Urban Areas Act of 1978. This expanded the existing UP and established three programme categories within which local agencies would enjoy enhanced economic powers and additional grants from central government. The new UP, like GEAR, focused on economic, environmental and social projects and it borrowed from the old UP a funding mechanism whereby local agencies, acting within central guidelines, would prepare a number of projects which were submitted annually to the department (Environment) for approval, the level of allocation being set centrally and the costs split 75:25 between central and local agencies. The most significant of the new categories— Partnerships—involved the creation of new institutional mechanisms similar to that used for GEAR. All relevant central departments plus both tiers of local government and the area health authorities were invited to send representatives to a Partnership Committee which was to co-ordinate the programme under the leadership of a Department of Environment Minister. Participation by local voluntary and private sector organisations was also welcomed. The limited, though significantly increased, resources available under the new UP were meant to provide a catalytic effect, and innovative projects pioneered through the programme were expected to acquire permanence via the "bending" of the main programmes of both tiers of government.

By 1979 then, the first year that the new UP was in operation, we find three different modes of urban economic policy-making, each combining a different mix of central and local actors and exhibiting varying levels of central control. At the most decentralised level, all local authorities, by no means only those seen to have "inner city" characteristics, were able to use limited specific powers and the general competence afforded by Section 137 to develop independent programmes largely free from central influence. Local expertise in economic development, including the growth of a proto-profession outside the established disciplines, became a feature in any authority where local political priorities willed it: no restrictions in either the substance of programmes or the areas in which they were developed were immediately available to the centre. Local authority experimentation was constrained, however, by limited statutory powers and finances and this led quickly to demands being placed on the centre by both individual councils and the local authority associations for enhanced local discretion.

The other two policy-making arenas were substantially similar to each other but reflect important differences in the structure of public administration between England and Scotland. Both the GEAR project and the new UP involved some decentralisation of decision-making to sub-national bodies but can equally be seen as attempts by the centre to regularise and control the policy process. Neither involved significant financial resources compared to the budgets of the local agencies involved, that is the SDA, local authorities and area health authorities. In the Scottish case there was no increase in the statutory resources of local participants whereas the new UP did offer local authorities greater scope in the provision of subsidies for site preparation, for treatment of land and buildings, for individual enterprises and for environmental works in new Industrial and Commercial Improvement Areas. The coverage of both programmes was selective, allowing the DoE (in England) and the Scottish Office to prioritise small areas in line with wider objectives, and to concentrate limited resources more effectively. Programming responsibilities were divided between departments (and, in Scotland, the SDA) and local agencies, so bringing decentralised agencies, and the interests represented in and by them, into the national policy process for the first time. The SDA took the lead in Scotland where suspicion on the part of departmental officials about the capacities of local authorities was more marked, whereas the new UP used local authorities as the lead agencies in programme preparation. In both cases it was hoped that the new initiatives would demonstrate central resolution in the tackling of urban economic decline whilst simultaneously establishing a framework within which decentralised agencies' priorities would converge with those of the centre. More ambitiously, it was hoped that the modest increase in statutory and financial resources, combined with the new organisational forms, would sensitise both central and local agencies to economic issues and result in main programmes being better related to local economic welfare. The late seventies therefore saw central government transform its approach to the inner cities issue and introduce a modest degree of pragmatic decentralisation which, if the resulting programmes were successful, would have had the effect of deflecting calls for a more thoroughgoing decentralist solution. Just how stable this "solution" might have proved is questionable: the Conservative victory in the 1979 election in any case made the question academic.

The Post-1979 Central Policy Environment

A detailed examination of the post-1979 initiatives will be necessary to assess whether the current system of policy-making is more centralised than the one which the Conservatives inherited. However it will be useful first to identify some of the underlying factors which have influenced the nature of policy under the Thatcher administrations. That central government policy survived in any form after 1979 may seem surprising. After all, the Conservatives were elected on a manifesto which promised sharply to reduce the level of governmental intervention in all spheres. In industrial policy terms this heralded moves towards a neo-classical minimal state role which would seek only to secure the general conditions for economic growth. Interventionist and corporatist bodies like the National Enterprise Board and the National Economic Development Council were scaled down or abolished, casting doubt on the survival of the SDA too, and there have been successive reductions in the coverage and scale of regional industrial assistance. There was also a commitment to sharp reductions in the size and scope of the public sector in the belief that the private provision of goods and services would be more efficient, and in line with national economic priorities for the curtailment of public expenditure. The budgets of local authorities and QGAs were particularly vulnerable in the latter regard.

Centrally-led urban economic development programmes have nevertheless grown in the last nine years for a number of reasons. At the most general level, the deep recession in the national economy, particularly in the first two years of Conservative control, significantly compounded urban economic decline: indeed the cities continued to suffer disproportionately in comparison to small town and rural areas and were less likely to benefit from any economic upturn.[4] The problem, therefore, did not disappear. The comparative novelty of the economic element of inner city policy, the fact that the UP in particular was untested, and the notoriously incremental nature of all public policy-making made immediate changes less likely. Compounding this was the fact that, despite an apparent commitment to free market solutions to economic problems, there survived within the Conservative Party a number

[4] For a brief analysis see Hasluck, C., *Urban Unemployment: Local Labour Markets and Employment Initiatives*, London: Longman, 1987, Chap. 3.

(including key DoE Secretaries of State) of "reluctant collectivists" who continued to advocate the need for public investment which would help the market to function. Such a view was more acceptable in this policy area since the idea of privatising urban development functions was a patent absurdity: public sector action was after all based on the failure of market mechanisms. Finally, and perhaps most important, a number of urban areas in England suffered serious outbreaks of rioting in 1981 and 1985, leading to intense pressure on the Government to step up its inner city initiatives.

If policy survival is unsurprising, so is the fact that the mechanisms used to deliver programmes changed. Again there are a number of contributory factors. Whilst the previous Labour government may have had reason to expect reasonable co-operation from urban local authorities due to the Party's electoral domination of urban areas, Conservative partnership with urban councils was likely to be less comfortable. The degree of central–local political conflict was heightened on the one side by a central strategy which sought to limit local authority expenditure and to restructure and decollectivise service delivery across a range of local government functions. Radicalised urban Labour councils, in which middle class, public sector professionals were increasingly influential,[5] resisted the central strategy fiercely and, particularly on financial issues, found themselves the target for increasingly draconian measures, thus heightening the conflict and further reducing the scope for joint working.

The changing composition of urban Labour parties radically affected economic policy orientations at the local level too. Underlying policy changes here was a desire to use local authorities as testing grounds in the development of alternative economic strategies which could be used both to resist the market-led policies of central government and to offer a lead to the national Labour Party. Disillusion with the remoteness and centralism of previous Labour initiatives; a desire to pursue traditional "socialist" concerns like furthering social ownership in industry and holding the private sector accountable for decisions on economic restructuring; the influence of the women's movement on issues involving the quality of and access to employment for groups which traditionally suffered disadvantage in the labour market; concern for the environmental effects of economic growth; all contributed to debates about what a progressive public sector role in the economy should entail and what was possible at the local level.

The decentralised policy-making arena referred to earlier was thus transformed and urban authorities began, within the limited resources available to them, to search for new policy instruments. Led by the metropolitan county councils and the larger districts in the aftermath of

---

[5] For a discussion of the changing membership and policy orientations of urban Labour Parties, see Gyford, J. *The Politics of Local Socialism*, London: Allen and Unwin, 1985, Chap. 2.

elections in the early 1980s which saw younger, more radical councillors rise to positions of prominence, urban councils soon developed distinctive localised economic strategies. The process was aided by the rapid dissemination of innovation through professional networks and the local authority associations. Although priorities differed between authorities, local concerns typically involved: a stress on the public sector role in urban regeneration; vigorous defence of public sector employment; forms of intervention in the private sector which would strengthen the position of workers within enterprises, encourage more democratic forms of ownership and control, provide long-term, secure employment in indigenous enterprises, promote equal opportunities in employment, and support the supply of "socially useful" goods and services; support for campaigning organisations such as trade union resource groups and centres for the unemployed; and the promotion of community involvement in economic planning.

This inevitably meant the creative use of limited resources. Whilst new policy statements were often highly ambitious, none of the authorities seriously believed that their independent efforts could provide solutions to local economic problems: rather their efforts were to be demonstrative. Section 137 continued to be the mainstay of independent programmes and, in those authorities which were supported by particularly large rate bases (the Greater London Council for example could raise £40 millions annually with this power), began to be used for significant innovations which could not be supported by other statutory powers. Foremost among these were the Enterprise Boards, established by a number of upper tier metropolitan authorities, which were independent venture capital companies offering assistance to new and existing enterprises subject to agreements on a range of issues. These might include worker involvement in management decisions, product ranges, unionisation, wage levels, training and other employment conditions. Attempts to improve employment conditions and worker organisation in the private sector were also made through the use of local authorities' bargaining powers as large scale contractors and purchasers. Contracts compliance procedures were developed, requesting information from suppliers and contractors and laying down council conditions for accepting tenders, in an attempt to reward firms with progressive employment policies. Firms found unacceptable in this regard, or for example because they had investments in South Africa, could be excluded from lists of contractors.

Much of the substance of the new, left-dominated urban council initiatives was a far cry from that of the earlier phase of local economic development and could not be pursued within the provisions of the UP. UP projects were incorporated as far as possible into local programmes but did not form an important strand of the new approach. Furthermore, the growing interest in using public sector power to influence private sector decisions on employment ran counter to Conservative government insistence on wage and labour flexibility and the erosion of trade union power.

A final contributory factor concerns the role of the SDA in urban regeneration. In the aftermath of the 1979 election the Agency, with its corporatist structure and interventionist functions, sat uneasily within the new set of governmental priorities. However the sensitivity of the Scottish Office to nationalist pressures which had helped push the Labour government into establishing the SDA in the first place, and the delicate political situation which saw Conservatives in a minority in Scotland, meant that governmental moves against the SDA were fraught with difficulty. In addition, the SDA had been unhappy with the way it had been precipitated by the Scottish Office into the lead role in GEAR (and later into two emergency projects which followed large scale industrial closures). Both issues were decisive in the Agency's developing role in the 1980s.

The Conservative Strategy

Conservative attempts to deal with the range of factors outlined above can be divided into three categories, all of which necessitated the extensive use of centralised powers. These were: attempts to limit the capacity of local authorities to pursue independent and potentially conflicting strategies; an increase in the influence of central departments in both those programmes which relied on central–local partnership and directly in implementation; and greater involvement of the private sector in policy formulation and implementation at the expense of established professional actors. Whereas the developing local authority strategies expressed concern, at least in principle, with the employment needs of local residents and the quality of employment in the private sector, central government put much greater emphasis on the physical dereliction of urban areas. With this as the primary concern, the role of the public sector was seen as providing, often in efforts limited to particular time-spans, the minimum necessary improvements for the private sector to be interested in developing sites. To the extent that labour was a factor at all, it was expected that private development would generate employment opportunities through a "trickle down" effect.

The use of Section 137 powers by local authorities has been subject to two separate reviews. The first, by the Burns Committee in 1982 resulted in a consultation document which proposed that selected urban areas be allowed to use the full rate product only to support small business formation and that other authorities be limited to just a halfpenny rate product. The document was withdrawn after the local authority associations, including those which were Conservative-dominated, made it clear that they were loath to surrender the only general power of competence available to them. The issue was reexamined by the Widdicombe Committee after allegations of the power being used to support "controversial" projects. The report failed to attach any substance to such suspicions, however, and defended the innovative way in which it had been used. No action has yet been taken on the subject but restrictions on, or the withdrawal of, Section 137 remain a possibility.

Local authority funding of economic development received its greatest blow when the Greater London Council and the six metropolitan county councils were abolished in 1986. Whilst it would be difficult to sustain the argument that abolition was motivated by the councils' experiments in economic development, it can nevertheless be seen in the context of the Government's arguments that these authorities, lacking in other substantial functions, had created roles for themselves which, it was asserted, trespassed on the legitimate functions of the centre and of lower tier authorities.[6] Metropolitan areas thereby lost the most innovative pursuers of economic development programmes and the lower tier authorities lost half of the Section 137 monies available citywide, previously targeted on the most depressed areas. Local authority influence on private sector employment conditions was diminished when contracts compliance procedures were outlawed in 1988 by legislation which forbade local authorities to place "non-economic" conditions on tenders.

Attempts to limit the influence of local authorities are also evident in changes which have been made to the local planning system. The announcement of the Enterprise Zone (EZ) experiment in 1980 was based on the unsubstantiated assertion that local planning procedures placed unnecessary restrictions on potential development. Under the Local Government (Planning and Land) Act of 1980, authorities became entitled to bid for the designation of the whole or part of their area, the boundaries being decided centrally, as an EZ. Plans for fixed categories of development are then drawn up by local authorities and, once ratified centrally, allow developers to proceed without the need to submit planning applications. Following initial planning decisions, local authorities therefore effectively lose planning control within EZs. Twenty-five authorities were nevertheless tempted into EZ designation between 1982 and 1984 largely because of the package of centrally-financed incentives, including rates holidays for firms, which are available within the zones, and the prospect of additional development which they held out.

A further White Paper on planning[7] extended the policy of deregulation. Initiatives arising from this include Simplified Planning Zones (SPZs) which received statutory underpinning in 1986. SPZs, similar to EZs but lacking the subsidy element, give local authorities the opportunity to publish a draft planning brief for a particular area which is then subject

[6] *Streamlining the Cities* Cmnd 9063, HMSO 1985, pp. 3–4.
[7] *Lifting the Burden* Cmnd 9571, London: HMSO, 1985.

to public consultation. Once accepted, developers are again permitted to proceed without planning permission. The Secretary of State can prescribe the procedure for SPZ designation and intervene in the detail, and local authorities are forced to consider proposals for designation from private developers. With no subsidy to tempt them, however, authorities have not been keen to use this process, and developers seem as yet to have decided that good relations with local planners through the established procedures are preferable to risking confrontation through the SPZ procedure. Changes were also made in the Use Classes Order which permits developers to apply directly to the Secretary of State for changes of use of buildings from light industrial to office use without referring to the local planning authority. This will have particular effect in those areas where councils have tried to protect industrial employment by preventing office development and the spiralling land costs which it tends to generate. In general, central government has tried to bend the planning process such that there is a routine presumption in favour of development. Other instruments which may be introduced include restrictions in the level of detail incorporated into local development plans and the introduction of time-limits for public enquiries.

Attempts to involve the private sector in policy formulation and implementation have built on a limited revival of "corporate social responsibility" in UK companies which attended the deepening economic crisis and the social disturbances in the cities.[8] Acting out of enlightened self-interest, a number of companies, fearing the social consequences of economic decline and wishing to cushion the effects of their own restructuring, developed a range of schemes to support local enterprise. Support for such schemes was offered by the Departments of Environment and Trade and Industry, and out of discussions on business-community relations came the formation in 1982 of Business in the Community (BIC), an umbrella organisation incorporating leading corporate executives and civil servants. ScotBIC, the Scottish sister organisation followed in 1983. With the help of regional DoE offices and the SDA these organisations have encouraged the formation of local Enterprise Agencies or Trusts which have attempted, with other local agencies, to offer a range of support services to small businesses.

Urban rioting in 1981 provided a further spur to this process. The Financial Institutions Group (FIG) was an *ad hoc* group of secondees from financial institutions hastily put together by the Secretary of State for the Environment following a famous bus tour of riot-torn Toxteth in Liverpool. Before disbanding in 1982, FIG convened a number of working groups which examined potential policy initiatives acceptable to the institutions. Out of these deliberations came the Urban Develop-

[8] See, for example, Richardson, J. J., Moore, C. and Moon, J. "Politicisation of Business: Corporate Response to Unemployment" (Paper to Politics and Business Workshop, ECPR, Barcelona, March 1985).

ment Grant (UDG) scheme in 1983. UDG allowed UP authorities to identify development schemes with the private sector wherein limited public investment, split 75:25 between central and local government, could "lever in" further private investment. Urban Regeneration Grant (URG), a modification of UDG whereby deals are struck directly between regional DoE offices and developers, was introduced in 1986 and the statutory involvement of local authorities in the process was eventually phased out completely when both schemes were merged into the new City Grant in 1988. Other FIG-inspired initiatives include the establishment, in 1983, of Inner City Enterprises, a property service company sponsored by financial institutions which seeks out and packages investment opportunities for individual developers. Powers were also taken to require local authorities to dispose of land at low cost.

The private sector has also been offered effective control over the major new institutional instruments developed by the Conservatives: Urban Development Corporations. Nine UDCs are now established in areas of significant dereliction. Financed from the Treasury, accountable directly to Parliament and run by appointees selected by the Secretary of State, UDCs take over development control functions from local authorities and have the power to acquire land compulsorily subject to statutory instruments. Local acquiescence has been ensured through appointing a minority of local councillors to UDC boards and by making it plain to local authorities that UDC designation and operations would go ahead irrespective of local reaction. In these circumstances local professional and political opposition has, with the exception of the London Docklands UDC, been muted and councils have been loath to be seen as resistant to the substantial influx of central funds, even though their influence over UDC action is slender and the development strategies they have tended to follow have offered little in the way of local employment opportunities.

Increased departmental influence over the policy process has come in two forms. Sixteen Task Forces, staffed by regional officials of the Departments of Environment, Employment, and Trade and Industry plus private sector secondees, have been set up in small sub-city areas since 1981 with a remit to take the lead in developing new projects across the range of departmental functions. Five interdepartmental City Action Teams have also been appointed in the cities covered by the Partnership programme with responsibility to develop projects and "improve the Government contribution to the Partnerships". DoE tutelage over the UP has also been increased in response to the dominance which local authorities wielded over programme content due to their control over information, and to Treasury worries over financial control mechanisms. Though the Partnerships in particular were supposed to involve other departments and local agencies, it has readily been accepted that the UP is little more than a bid by local authorities for project funding from the DoE. The idea that agencies should "bend" main programme expenditure quickly became irrelevant as public expenditure cuts were imposed throughout the 1980s. New Ministerial guidelines for the UP stressed the development of the economic side of the programme and required authorities to consult local Chambers of Commerce on its contents whilst the Urban Programme Management initiative (UPM) was introduced in 1985 to improve the information flowing from the localities to the centre. The DoE also appraises every project submitted in the UP.

Against this experiment of centralisation, the situation in Scotland, and to some extent in Wales, has been slightly less destructive of the role of decentralised agencies. The SDA has managed, with the support of the Scottish Office, to tread a delicate path between independence and conformity to central policy. From 1979 the Agency developed its own programme of urban projects in which it has concluded voluntary agreements with local and regional councils on the substance and timetabling of action. Integrated projects have been set up in six further areas and the Agency, whilst being the dominant partner for the duration of each project, has tried to ensure that local authorities along with the private sector through Enterprise Trusts, maintain momentum after the Agency withdraws.

In conclusion then, we see a significant shift along the continuum towards centralisation since 1979. Central government has used its legislative supremacy to constrain independent local authority initiatives and to limit local control over the development process. Legislative and administrative power has also been used significantly to extend the role of central departments, centrally-appointed agencies and the private sector in the formulation and implementation of urban economic development policy. Acceptance, however reluctant, of new agencies and programmes by local elected bodies has been smoothed by the injection of financial resources which otherwise would not have been available. Central tutelage over programmes relying on intergovernmental partnership has also been extended. There are modifying factors though. The decentralised nature of the SDA (and the WDA, its Welsh counterpart) and its accountability to a department which itself has territorial responsibilities, combined with a particular set of national political characteristics and shrewdness in Agency leadership, has meant that Scotland has escaped some of the worst features of English centralisation. In England too, the human and informational resources available to local authorities mean that the centre must concede some influence to them, particularly in the UP but also in the way the Task Forces work and even to some extent in the operations of UDCs. The limited response of the private sector to central initiatives, and occasional concerted action by the local authority associations, has also helped in the retention of some decentralised discretion.

Is Centralisation Inevitable?

In general, we can see that central government in Britain in the last nine years has been able to use a combination of legislative, financial, physical and human resources to extend its own influence over the policy process, to change the mix of interests represented in and influencing policy decisions, and to constrain those actions of decentralised agencies which were seen as inconsistent with central objectives. Whilst central reliance on decentralised agencies for implementation means that central control is less than total, it cannot seriously be argued that current policy-making is not more centralised than previously, even allowing for the limited decentralism before this time. The question which remains is whether this is an inevitable feature of British public administration.

Central involvement in urban economic development programmes continues to be necessary for two prinicipal reasons. The levels of investment required are such that local agencies cannot provide the resources independently. Central sponsorship is therefore needed in order to prevent the anomalous situation whereby areas with high need have low financial capacity to sponsor programmes, whereas those with low need have high capacity. Central involvement is also needed to balance territorial demands such that they are consistent with wider, national priorities. On occasion this will mean constraints being imposed on high growth areas, possibly in contravention of local agency wishes. There may also be occasional need to encourage local agencies to develop programmes where this would not otherwise have happened. Beyond these factors the level of centralisation depends on the structure of government and its impact on policy-making, and on party political factors.

Recent Conservative governments have clearly decided that the issue of urban development is a sufficiently high priority, and the politics of central–local relations sufficiently intractable, that physical regeneration programmes need, in many circumstances, to be pushed through with little regard to the involvement or priorities of local elected agencies. Even to the extent that these programmes are successful there is little indication that the underlying problem of high concentrations of urban unemployment, in both inner cities and peripheral public housing estates, will diminish. Neither is it likely that the influx of more affluent workers into urban areas which these policies have encouraged will be sufficient to change urban voting patterns radically.

Whilst the character of the inner-city problem may change, it is unlikely that its salience will diminish or that intergovernmental politics will change drastically. The short term may well see two developments. First there will be pressure on the centre to ensure that some of the benefits of development are passed on to disadvantaged inner city residents. On this issue there may be some room for agreement with urban councils. However, local democratic participation in policy decisions remains unlikely. Economic development is a comparatively minor issue in central–local relations and it would be surprising if Conservative determination to restructure the welfare state, by removing service responsibilities from local authorities in much more significant expenditure areas like housing and education, did not continue to generate conflicts which will dominate relations with local authorities. For this reason mechanisms which rely on partnership are unlikely to be welcomed by the Government. The use of other agencies such as the Training Agency, now suitably restructured to diminish local council and trade union influence, is more likely. Secondly, and slightly modifying this scenario, there is evidence that urban authorities, in the absence of any other option, will reluctantly adopt pragmatic responses to central economic development programmes and attempt to use the limited influence they have in damage limitation strategies. This is a predictable result of urban councils' willingness to oppose central initiatives and to develop radical alternatives having been destroyed by the experience of recent years.

Continued centralisation in the short term, even where there is an apparent willingness by local councils to co-operate, is therefore likely for political reasons. Even if we assume the medium term election of an administration likely to look more positively on Labour-dominated urban councils, a decentralist strategy does not follow. We have seen that the era of non-partisan inner city policy during the 1970s, and the reform of the UP by a Labour government, resulted only in limited decentralisation. Since then we have seen how a number of urban councils experimented in local economic strategies with the explicit aim of demonstrating the value of decentralised programmes to the national leadership. Along with the proponents of regional government, the supporters of local authority initiatives form a significant lobby within the Labour Party but their influence is questionable. Despite the emergence of one or two figures from local government on to the national political scene, there continues to be a rigid separation between national and local elites in Labour politics, leading the party to overemphasise the use of centralised powers.

The fiasco over devolution for Scotland and Wales in the 1970s was one case in point, and the ease with which the national leadership can manipulate and ignore local pressures was shown again in the run-up to the last election. Support for independent local authority programmes was then at its peak, following the recent abolition of the upper tier metropolitan authorities. Labour was also desperate to show nationally that it had a credible policy for reducing unemployment. Invitations were therefore extended to local authorities to prepare emergency job-creation plans which could assist this effort and form the basis of new programmes should the election result prove favourable. The result was that the innovative elements of local strategies were forgotten by a number of councils which saw an opportunity simply to bid for massive growth in local authority employment. The resulting "jobs plans" were nevertheless publicised heavily by the national party until it became apparent that the climate of public hostility to local authorities made the effort counter-productive. Emphasis then switched to employment creation in more popular public services.

Such events are indicative of deeper tensions between the local wings of the Labour Party which make coherent policies on the institutional reform of government and the extent of decentralisation in economic policy-making difficult to establish. Whilst crystal-ball gazing on Labour policy is a difficult exercise at the best times (and predictions of electoral success even more hazardous), it must be said that plans for the creation of an all-purpose single tier of local authorities overlaid by regional government, and for a framework of economic planning in which regional agencies and local authorities play a part are at a formative stage[9] and excite little enthusiasm within the party as a whole. There is in any case little likelihood that a further round of local governmental reform would be an immediate priority come the next change of government. In these circumstances the use of established policy mechanisms would seem to be the most likely option, and this could entail limited decentralisation. Spending restrictions under Section 137 might be relaxed, and localised investment agencies established by offering specific powers to urban authorities or recreating the SDA model in selected English regions. A mechanism similar to the UP by which local authorities make annual bids as part of a large scale rolling programme for economic development may also be favoured. Despite the evidence across Europe, and particularly through the work of the European Commission, that supra-national and regional economic policy-making are likely to assume more importance in comparison to national strategies, it is as yet difficult to be sanguine about the prospects for a more decentralised system of urban economic policy-making in Britain.

[9] Interested readers should consult Labour Parliamentary Spokesman's Working Group *Alternative Regional Strategy: A Framework for Discussion*, London: Labour Party 1982, and *Real Needs—Local Jobs*, London: Labour Party, 1987, plus Labour Party Consultative Paper *Local Government Reform in England and Wales*, London: Labour Party, 1987, at their leisure.

THOUGHTS ON THE UNION BETWEEN LAW AND OPINION *OR* DICEY'S LAST STAND

CHRISTOPHER HARVIE*

AFTER a recent interview Gordon Wilson, Chairman of the Scottish National Party, recollected travelling to London about 1979 in the company of a senior Home Office bureaucrat, who told him that in 1976 the Home Office had plans to transfer police north, in case public order in Scotland broke down after rebellious MPs had forced the withdrawal of the Scotland and Wales Act. "That just shows," he said, "how little they understand us." In other words, the Scots might be turning nationalist, but no way were they going to replicate the way most other nationalists, even in Western Europe, went about achieving self-determination.[1]

Hugh MacDiarmid once wrote that "the absence of Scottish nationalism is, paradoxically enough, a form of Scottish self-determination".[2] In the sense that nationalism is *about* uniqueness, this phenomenon has simultaneously weakened and strengthened Scots identity. Now that a movement for autonomy has emerged, and the desire for a legislature embraces about 80% of the Scots electorate, the paradox has advanced. Defined in terms of party programmes the movement is completely parliamentary and, until very recently, has foresworn the appeal to direct action conjured up elsewhere in Europe. As Neal Ascherson observed in 1977:

> There is no tradition here of what one might call "intermediate direct action", of sitting down in the street or not paying taxes or letting down government tyres or covering dignitaries with dye . . . in general only two courses are perceived. One is the ultra-correct suit-and-tie Westminster approach through the appropriate democratic channels. (but) What do the Scots do, however, if they are rewarded with an invitation to piss off and shut up? This is where the lack of political resourcefulness becomes alarming. The only other course understood by the national imagination is violence.[3]

* Professor in British Studies at the University of Tübingen in West Germany whose works include *No Gods and Precious Few Heroes: Scotland since 1914*, the final volume in Edward Arnold's *New History of Scotland*, 1981, revised 1987, and a Fabian tract *Against Metropolis*, 1982. An earlier version of this paper appeared in A. Macartney's *Self-Determination in the Commonwealth Context*, Aberdeen U.P., 1987.

[1] Gordon Wilson, interview with C. T. Harvie in September 1986.
[2] *Albyn, or Scotland and the Future*, Routledge, London, 1927, p. 46.
[3] "Devolution Diary" in *Cencrastus*, Spring 1986, p. 8.

Ascherson may have been over-persuaded by Polish parallels: seeing the shadow of the Warsaw uprising in what he admits were the idiocies of the Army of the Provisional Government, whose caperings masked nothing sinister or significant. In the early eighties research on the direct action issue suggested that a bit of shouting was the most the Scots would allow themselves:

> One obvious characteristic of political violence in Britain is its low level in Scotland . . . . support for direct action was always less, much less, than the number who would endorse the general principle of direct action.[4]

Least of all, it seemed, for the cause of political autonomy.

How do we account for the deep structure of legalism in the Scottish political psyche? Although Scotland has a history of repression amounting at times to state terror, with victims ranging from Jacobites after 1745 and Jacobins after 1793 to the likes of John MacLean in World War I, law has been accepted as something more than an instrument for the settlement of institutional and social conflicts.[5] The fact that the present Scottish political leadership is almost monopolised by lawyers reflects their centrality to civil society. Legalism is congruent with the other conventions—the monarchy, the party structure—of the Union.

It is an accepted fact that these conventions are now loosening, notoriously because of the desire of a highly-ideological centralising government to dismantle any power-centres which conflict with its aims, but also as the result of direct, or at least extra-parliamentary action on the British periphery. Sabotage and hunger strikes—or the threat of them—have played some part in securing privileges for the Welsh language. The pressure exerted by the Catholic minority in Northern Ireland has caused an unprecedented dilution of parliamentary sovereignty in the case of the Anglo-Irish Agreement. Yet, despite all this, Scots legalism has only very recently and, so far, very tentatively, been challenged—over the issue of the poll tax. And here the divisions between "legalists" and "rebels" can sometimes seem deeper than those between Conservatives and home rulers.[6]

Scottish legalism seems quixotically out of synchronisation with the rest of the British periphery and its intellectual elites. The gaining of the Welsh-language TV channel has compensated for the political catastrophe of 1979. In Northern Ireland the troubles since 1968 have claimed a horrific cost, but they have provoked an unparalleled and ecumenical cultural resurgence, particularly evident in poetry and the drama, which may provide the necessary psychological underpinning for an Ulster "identity" consonant with the Anglo–Irish Agreement of 1985.[7] Scotland

---

[4] William L. Miller, "Support for Direct Action in Scotland", Strathclyde University Politics Department, Sept. 1981.

[5] Harvie, "Legalism, Myth and National Identity in Scotland in the Imperial Epoch" in *Cencrastus*, Summer 1987 (No. 26), pp. 35–41.

[6] Jim Sillars, interview with C. T. Harvie, 3 October 1986.

[7] See, for example, John Osmond, *The National Question Again: Welsh Political*

has had a comparable revival in literary and artistic life since 1979, with significant achievements in film and the novel and, as elsewhere, a major expansion of historical and cultural studies. Moreover, the emphasis in this revival has been on post-industrial social evolution, and has been accompanied, among the intelligentsia—a newish concept in 1968—by a detachment bordering upon almost complete contempt for the traditional metropolitan arbiters of British culture.[8] "Britishness", in fact, has now ceased to be an accepted condition of political life and become a problem to be externalised and analysed. The Falklands war, for example, awoke little popular enthusiasm on the periphery, and the intellectual response to it was overwhelmingly hostile to the British government. Tam Dalyell, who had not scrupled to call Hugh Trevor-Roper to his side in 1977, was redeemed by his implacable hostility to the war. In fact, by 1988, for a native to invoke any such London literary gent to pronounce on Scottish affairs would seem incredible.[9]

Of course, this evaluation flatters the intellectuals. In the 1970s the Gramscian left in Scotland certainly over-valued its thaumaturgic powers, as indeed did those 1968ers who set People's Democracy in motion in Ulster. "What we think we can," wrote (thirty years earlier) the Ulsterman Louis MacNeice, "the old idealist lie". In Ulster the punters took cover from the gunmen, or in Scotland just lost interest. But the question remains important because some sort of ruling ideas direct the thought of those trying to make sense of social reality, and it does seem that the ideas being bandied about on the British periphery— even Scottish legalism—are more disparate than they ought to be, in a state which, if federalised, will require a range of strong common institutions and procedures.[10]

The British literary elite, Noel Annan's "intellectual aristocracy"— a ponderous liberal cousinhood—has plainly taken a battering from economic decline, social tension and the dynamic simplicities of Thatcherism, and some remarkable mutations among *ci-devant* herbivores have emerged. Leaving aside the professional hysterics and clowns, one wing has found salvation in the 'liberal' economy, and indulges in Rubashov-like self-accusation about its anti-industrial, anti-entrepreneurial past; the other condemns Thatcher and all her works, refuses her an honorary degree and curses the City and Rupert Murdoch from

Identity in the 1980s, Gomer, Cardiff, 1985, and Tom Paulin, *Ireland and the English Crisis*, Bloodaxe, Belfast, 1984.

[8] Tom Nairn, *The Break-up of Britain*, New Left Books, London, 1977, *passim*.

[9] The most recent example of this is Tom Nairn's *The Enchanted Glass: Britain and its Monarchy*, Radius Hutchinson, London, 1988; and see also Cairns Craig, "George Orwell and the English Ideology"; Angus Calder, "The Myth of the Blitz" in *Cencrastus* 16, Spring 1984. Alan Massie's novel *One Night in Winter*, Bodley Head, London, 1984, is one of the few attempts at a Tory novel on contemporary Scottish politics.

[10] In federal West Germany, for example, there is a much greater sense of common political, educational and religious values than in the UK. It is, for instance, characteristic for party leaders to shift politicians from Land to Land, something unheard of in Britain.

behind its William Morris chintzes. Is anyone in Scotland listening to either?[11]

Fifty years ago some Scots fitted into both the Scots and the metropolitan intelligentsia: men such as John Buchan or Walter Elliot, James Bridie or Eric Linklater. There are a few Welsh or Northern Irish equivalents—Tom Jones, Goronwy Rees, Joyce Cary, Robert Lynd and St John Ervine. "Dual nationality" John Mackintosh—one of its more radical representatives—called this assumption of a solid agricultural and industrial society, broadly congruent throughout the kingdoms, defining itself through its imperial responsibilities and sponsorship of "British values", Betjeman's

> Free speech, free passes, class distinction,
> Democracy and proper drains.

This "Britishness" was not marginal to constitutional issues: Disraeli wrote in 1835 that "the foundation of civil polity is Convention" and his successors in the politico–literary intelligentsia have been the Guardians of the Ark of the Unquestioned. In present circumstances, their task is, however, no easy one.[12]

Constitutional Conventions

Political ideology, the dynamism of international finance capital and intellectual divergence has intruded the incalculable into British constitutional relationships. Policy towards Northern Ireland has created precedents implying that minorities within the United Kingdom have the right to decide on their relationship to England (The Northern Ireland Constitution Act of 1973 conferred a right of self-determination ascertained through plebiscite, and a Constitutional Convention was elected in 1975).[13] At the same time the notion that devolution of power to Scotland could simply be policed by constitutional conventions has taken a battering through the actuality of direct rule in Ulster and the government's assault on the autonomy and indeed existence of local government in England.

But if governments now disregard the "rules of the game", *British* public consent to the authoritarian administration of troublesome peripheral populations is not inexhaustible. Most British voters want to pull out of Northern Ireland, regardless of the risks, and violent opposition to London rule in Scotland would probably produce a similar

[11] See Michael Frayn, "Festival" in Sissons and French, eds., *The Age of Austerity*, 1963, Penguin, Harmondsworth, 1964, p. 331; and see C. T. Harvie, "Liturgies of National Decadence' in *Cencrastus*, Summer 1985.

[12] Disraeli, *A Vindication of the English Constitution* (London, 1835), Ch. 5.

[13] Kevin Boyle, "The Anglo–Irish Agreement, 1985: Differing Perceptions, Differing Realities" in W. J. Allan Macartney, ed., *Self-Determination in the Commonwealth*, Aberdeen University Press, 1988, pp. 91–99.

reaction. To date a majority of Scots, when polled, still subscribe to Mackintosh's "dual nationality", but that figure (expressed as '*status quo*'+'devolution') has gone down pretty steeply since the 1970s, from over 75% to under 66%. The number of Labour voters in the 'independence' camp, and the number who might transfer to the SNP, suggests that this could in future become the most important, if not the majority, political option.[14]

This is the ideological background against which, since 1979, a Conservative government, endorsed by only 24% of the Scots electorate, has administered Scotland. In a Scottish context, it has had no mandate for the dismantling of regional economic aid in 1984, nor for the imposition of a regressive "community charge" as a substitute for rates. The usual response by Westminster to this argument is that the majority of Scots Labour voters are content to keep a British Labour government in power, although it may enjoy only a minority support in England. Yet how far, nowadays, do such conventions really count for anything?

Conventions, by their very nature, are subjective. What, to A, is binding, is to B a legal fiction. Many Scots, for example, hold that there is a strictly constitutional approach to the Scottish issue. This assumes that the Act of Union of 1707 was a fundamental law, which Parliament could not, subsequently, alter, and which, because it guaranteed specific Scottish institutions—Church, law, education, etc.—was open to "positive" interpretation by them. Thus, as regards Anglo–Scottish relations, Parliament was *not* sovereign but had to act with due cognizance of Scottish interests. Since, almost immediately after the Union, Parliament abolished the Scottish Privy Council and passed the Patronage act, both of which were against the terms of the Act of Union, this assumption may seem fanciful, but *ideologically* it embedded itself deeply, particularly on the Tory side, while it seemed *practically* to be recognised by eighteenth century government in which, as Nicholas Phillipson writes,

> the constitutional basis of this state of semi-independence lay in the act of Union . . . buttressed by the various arrangements and improvisations which gave to Scotland her own system of collecting revenue and her own court of exchequer and which, for most of the century, left the ordinary business of government to a manager . . .[15]

Plainly, when Sir Walter Scott and the *Blackwoods*' Tories talked of assaults on the Constitution, as in the Malagrowther pamphlets (1826) or in squibs like Aytoun's "The Dreepdailly Burghs" (1847) they had this Anglo–Scottish relationship in mind. When the Duke of Argyll, in

---

[14] System Three Poll in the *Glasgow Herald* (Assembly 46%, Complete Independence 34%, No Change 20%) see *Herald*, 5 May 1986.

[15] N. T. Phillipson, "Nationalism and Ideology" in J. N. Wolfe, ed., *Government and Nationalism in Scotland*, Edinburgh University Press, 1969, pp., 168–9.

the 1830s a Tory follower of Peel, surveyed the Church crisis of 1834–43, he commented:

> I have never yet met an Englishman who could understand, or even conceive, that idea of the relations between Church and State which was embedded and embodied in the Constitution of Scotland.[16]

The "Scottish Constitution" was seen, by Argyll as by Thomas Chalmers, as a defence against Benthamite-Jacobin centralisation. This Tory attitude may also account for the party affiliation of John Galt, in most other aspects a radical. Mr Selby, a semi-autobiographical figure in his political novel *The Member* (1832) is given the lines:

> Till Governments, and Houses of Commons, and those institutions which the sinful condition of man renders necessary, are made responsible to a tribunal of appeal, whose decisions shall control them, there can be no effectual reform. The first step is to take away all will of its own from Government—for statesmen are but men, rarely in talent above the average of their species, from what I have seen—and oblige it to consider itself no better than an individual, even with respect to its own individual subjects. Let the Law in all aspects be paramount, and it will matter little whether the lords or the vagabonds send members to Parliament . . .[17]

To say this is not to enlist any of the above as home rulers, but to suggest that Scottish Tories saw the Act of Union as something that offered fixed guarantees to Scotland within the Union, and not the creation of the dynamic instrument of a sovereign parliament. This attitude lasted. In his novel *Witch Wood* (1928) John Buchan gave the Marquess of Montrose the lines:

> There is but one master in the land, and its name is Law—which is in itself a creation of a free people under the inspiration of the Almighty. That law may be changed by the people's will, but till it be so changed it is to be revered and obeyed. It has ordained the King's prerogative, the rights of the subject, and the rights and duties of the Kirk. The state is like the body, whose health is only to be maintained by a just proportion among its members. If a man's belly be his god, his limbs will suffer; if he use only his legs, his arms will dwindle. If, therefore, the King should intrude upon the subject's rights, or the subject whittle at the King's prerogative, or the Kirk set herself above the Crown, there will be a sick state and an ailing people.[18]

Montrose, he wrote in his formal biography (1929), contributed ideals which "are in the warp and woof of the constitutional fabric of today".[19] In providing this dramatic *caesura* between the seventeenth and twentieth centuries, Buchan may have had in mind his friend F. S.

---

[16] Duke of Argyll, *Autobiography*, John Murray, London, 1906, p. 174.

[17] John Galt, *The Member*, 1832, Scottish Academic Press, Edinburgh, 1975, p. 62.

[18] John Buchan, *Witch Wood*, Hodder and Stoughton, London, 1928, p. 69.

[19] quoted in S. Buchan, ed., *The Clearing House*, Hodder and Stoughton, London, 1966, p. 54.

Oliver, who had in 1912 as a member of the Round Table group suggested the creation of a formal federal constitution for the British Isles. At any rate when another Tory, Lord Cooper, pronounced in 1953 that parliamentary sovereignty was "a distinctively English principle which has no part in Scottish constitutional law", he could draw on a wealth of precedent.[20]

Insofar as the Union preserved the autonomy of the Scottish courts, a traditional stamping ground of the gentry, the Tory tradition held good. Whigs and utilitarians were much more sceptical. Henry Cockburn denounced the old vestiges of Scottish autonomy—"corruption for the sake of faction was their sole effect"—as mere implements of patronage.[21] These were anyway bound to fall victim to the reform of Parliament and central administration which replaced a politics of patronage by a politics of incorporation, but the Tory tradition undoubtedly combined with radical distrust of overmuch centralisation to help produce the settlement of 1885.[22]

Utilitarian Paradoxes

1885–6 saw the re-creation of the Scottish Secretaryship; those years also saw a sharp economic slump, the East End wrecking London clubland, and Gladstone attempting—with prescience but not with success—to grant home rule to Ireland. All such threats were overcome, and the seal was set on Parliament triumphant by the acclaim granted Albert Venn Dicey's thesis of the absolute supremacy of Parliament, emphatically conveyed by *The Law of the Constitution*.[23]

Dicey, Vinerian Professor of Law at Oxford, called himself "the prophet of the obvious". A shambling, intellectually limited, but engagingly self-aware figure, he wrote with an energy and limpidity which lodged his ideas in the English political mind for decades, and was also at the very centre of the "intellectual aristocracy".[24] Dicey became a militant Unionist, convinced (despite a sympathy for the nationalist aspirations of the Irish) that any step towards federalism would destroy the British political stability he dated from the Anglo–Scottish Union. But this conversion was close-run. From his correspondence with his friend, the home ruler James Bryce, and the articles he wrote for the

[20] quoted in J. G. Kellas, *Modern Scotland*, Pall Mall, London, 1968, p. 103.

[21] Henry Cockburn, *Journal*, Edmonstone, Edinburgh, 1874, p. 35, quoted in Athole L. Murray, "Administration and Law" in T. I. Rae, *The Union of 1707*, Blackie, Glasgow, 1974, p. 55.

[22] See H. C. G. Matthew, "Disraeli, Gladstone and the Politics of mid-Victorian Budgets" in *Historical Journal*, Vol. XXII (1979), No. 3; and H. C. G. Matthew, "Introduction" to *The Gladstone Diaries, 1868–71*, Oxford University Press, 1982, p. xxx.

[23] See C. T. Harvie, *The Lights of Liberalism: University Liberals and the Challenge of Democracy*, Allen Lane, Harmondsworth, 1976, p. 230.

[24] Richard A. Cosgrove, *The Rule of Law: Albert Venn Dicey, Victorian Jurist*, Macmillan, London, 1980, p. 298.

New York *Nation*, it is obvious that, had Parliament voted for it in 1886, he would have acquiesced in home rule and a written constitution.[25] Instead, the "aged and impenitent Benthamite" discovered that parliamentary sovereignty provided a very efficient vehicle for the extension of the authority of the State. In *Law and Public Opinion in the 19th Century*, lectures which he delivered at Harvard in 1898, he deprecated the lapse from an individualism which he regarded as "utterly and absolutely right", but saw the trend towards collectivism as inevitable.

Now, the relevance of Dicey to the present crisis is this. If the possibility of a participative, pluralist democracy threatened in 1886 to bring parliamentary sovereignty to an end, what criteria for the performance of government could be evolved which would preserve it? This reopened a problem central to utilitarian political morality: the compatibility—or lack of it—between securing the greatest good to the greatest number and, to this end, inflicting harm on the minority. Dicey's friend Henry Sidgwick had approached an inverted version of this problem. If enlightened self-interest was the basis of utilitarian ethical calculation then, he asked, what rule of conduct was to be followed when the greatest good could only be obtained by personal self-sacrifice? Sidgwick could see no alternative to a first-line adherence to "duties"; "politics" occurred where these had to give way to utilitarian calculation.[26] But the existence of duties required the recognition of rights. To illustrate this from Dicey's "period of Benthamism or Individualism, 1830–1870", the government secured social benefits to the majority by discriminating against the rural poor and against the Irish. In the latter case the result was a retaliatory renunciation of citizenship and, psychologically at least, a withdrawal of consent, while in the former case Dicey admitted that the rigour of Benthamism was checked by the "counter current" of philanthropic social reform. Embodied by Lord Shaftesbury and the "social novelists"— Dickens, Mrs Gaskell, etc.—this consciousness of "rights" played a major part in amending "Benthamism or Individualism" to "the Age of Collectivism" after 1870.[27]

Dicey had realised, by 1898, that the appropriate guarantee for his political community was social welfare. As a good utilitarian, he had dismissed ideas of "rights" as so much nonsense, but he could see that household suffrage, granted in 1884, was bringing such demands in its wake. Benthamism "had forged the arms most needed by socialists". In *Law and Opinion* he performed an unwieldy gyration, approving the idea of an innate right as a bulwark against "the tyranny of majority" (but not examining the "rights", say, of the Irish *vis à vis* the majority

[25] C. T. Harvie, "Ideology and Home Rule: James Bryce, A. V. Dicey and Ireland, 1880–87" in the *English Historical Review*, 1976, pp. 298–314.

[26] Henry Sidgwick, *The Methods of Ethics*, Macmillan, London, 1874, pp. 460ff.

[27] A. V. Dicey, *Law and Public Opinion*, Macmillan, London, 1905, p. 243.

English). Reluctantly he had to admit that, on balance, it would be better to concede to collectivist demands than to court the diplomatic and constitutional difficulties incidental to home rule.[28]

Dicey's *Law of the Constitution* is a pro-parliamentary tract which works on the parliamentary principle of the frequent repetition of a simple proposition. In contrast with subsequent treatments, however, it is a work of austere reason. Sir Ivor Jennings' *The British Constitution*, which ran into five editions between its first publication in 1941 and Jennings' death in 1966, is a hymn to the imagination in politics which roots its analysis—and indeed half its length—in the stability of the two-party system. "Liberty", writes Jennings,

> is a consequence not of laws but of an attitude of mind . . . The symbol of liberty is Her Majesty's opposition.[29]

Jennings insists that

> the action of the State must be directed to achieve the happiness and prosperity of all sections of the community, without regard to wealth, social prestige, 'race' or religion.[30]

But if the guarantees of this—an impartial judiciary and the party system—looked debatable in 1966, they seem all but fraudulent in 1989. This is not just on account of the right-wing identification of the judiciary (intervening on an unprecedented scale in political and social questions); but because such interventions can only clarify statutes when in collision with each other or with earlier judicial decisions; they cannot measure them against any logical code of "rights". A decision of this sort *is* (within limits) possible, but only by going to the European Court of Justice, and the political implication of this is to make the British judiciary identify even more closely with the British state.

As for conventions of parliament, these were completely bound up with the expectations entertained of the party system: that it would consist of two competing parliamentary elites enjoying between them 90–95% electoral support, and manipulating their extra-parliamentary organisations from a consensual centre. Regional heterogeneity was not foreseen, nor was the fall in the two-party strength to 75% or less, with its disproportionate impact on the division of constituencies. The implications for the Labour Party of the "post-industrial" break-up of the traditional class-system were underestimated, as was the ease with which, in such circumstances, an essentially authoritarian organisation like the Conservative Party could transform itself into a fusion of state-and-party disturbingly similar to some aspects of the inter-war European "radical right".

The point to grasp is that this "poetic constitutionalism" is essentially the creation of British social democracy: a Fabian appropriation of the

---

[28] *Ibid*, "Introduction" to second edition, 1919, pp. xxiii–xciv.
[29] Jennings, *op. cit.*, Cambridge University Press, 1966, pp. 203, 206.
[30] *Ibid.*, p. 205.

state in the interests of social interventionism—never mind that its basis of popular consent lay in sociological suppositions about political behaviour rather than a hard-and-fact notion of "rights". This is observable in the qualitative decline of Harold Laski, from the acuteness of his *Studies in the Problem of Sovereignty* (1916) with its pluralistic critique of the "overmighty" British state, to a position virtually indistinguishable from that of Jennings. Yet, as the Dicey–Sidgwick issue indicates, some concept of "rights" was inevitable and, insofar as the theorists of the British welfare state ever grasped at ideology—rarely enough—they saw welfare rights, worked out and conceded by the administrative elite, as an alternative to the individual or group-right to participate in government. The Oxford-educated William Beveridge, who as civil service head of the Ministry of Munitions crushed the labour aristocrats of the Red Clyde (to whom their "rights" were much more important than their Marxism) in 1916, was the same man who transformed Roosevelt's moral imperatives into "the right to welfare" in 1942.[31]

Participatory rights did not achieve a high profile among British social democrats of the 1950s or 1960s. One of the most influential, Anthony Crosland, essentially argued that a disciplined mixed economy would consolidate its social dividends as rights to full employment, sex equality, improved education, state pensions, etc.—and that these, universally and uniformly available, would cement the already solid conventions of the two-party system. The securing of equality of access to those rights, rather than the devolution to communities of decisions about what rights they actually wanted, marked the general approach of that Butskellite elite whose "effortless superiority" was so salient until the mid-1960s. The only inter-party difference was that the Conservatives were more willing than Labour to allow freedom of action to local elites.[32]

A critical example is Northern Ireland after 1945. The major gulf which opened up between it and Eire was less the latter's republicanism, the Border question or the privileges of the Catholic Church than the fact that the British government's financial inputs during World War II led to more-or-less full employment in Northern Ireland. This, and the welfare state, pushed *per capita* income up to almost 175% of that in the Republic of Ireland by 1950, compared with about 105% pre-war. The "rights" which purchased consent to partition were welfare rights, and what triggered the collapse of the system in 1969 were inequities in the allocation of these rights—in housing—which the conventions of Westminster–Stormont relationships had hitherto tolerated.[33]

---

[31] José Harris, *William Beveridge*, Oxford University Press, 1977, pp. 222–3.

[32] Cf. Anthony Crosland, "The Transition from Capitalism" in *New Fabian Essays*, 1952, Dent, London, 1970, pp. 33–68; and see Stephen Haseler, *The Gaitskellites*, Macmillan, London, 1969, p. 85.

[33] David Johnson, The Interwar Economy in Ireland: Studies in Irish Economic and Social History, No. 4, Dublin, 1985, p. 43.

Citizenship and Welfare

Any welfare definition of citizenship rights must relate them closely to legislative programmes, administrative institutions and party philosophy. James Bulpitt had shown how this became a Conservative philosophy of "central autonomy" in the years after 1886.[34] While Government busied itself with "real" or "high" politics—foreign policy, etc.—local elites were left to manage "welfare" after a consensus fashion, something consonant with Dicey's commendation of Scottish political practice. This example of national interests being respected by the Union[35] involved a degree of wishful thinking, as any consensus became increasingly difficult to achieve, given the divisions which opened up in church and society in nineteenth century Scotland.[36] But the creation of the Scottish Secretaryship in 1885, by agreement between the two main parties, could be seen as an attempt to rectify this dysfunction, and produce an institution appropriate to the succeeding "period of collectivism". While the Irish Viceroy and the Chief Secretary existed to impose British rule on Ireland, the Scottish Secretary was supposed to represent a Scottish interest, to conciliate Scottish opinion and organise consent for legislation among the Scottish institutions. The occasion of his creation in fact coincided with a major government intervention directed at curbing freedom of contract—the Land Act of 1886—in which particular "welfare" rights were conceded to highland crofters, and the further expansion of his powers, into lowland agriculture in 1910 and urban housing in 1919, reinforced this principle.[37]

In this context two conventions secured the acquiescence of the Scots in the system of devolved administration. The first was that Scots interests and institutions were involved in determining and executing government policy. This principle—consonant with "central autonomy"—can be seen, for example, in the extension of the Secretary of State's powers into economic affairs in the 1930s and 1940s. The Scottish Economic Committee of 1935, a quango funded by the "Scottish Commissioner" under the Special Areas Act of 1934, had a predominant representation of industrialists, largely drawn from the Scottish National Development Council (a body created by resolution of the Convention of Royal Burghs in 1930) but also (uniquely in Britain) about a quarter of its members represented organised labour and its political represen-

[34] Bulpitt, "Conservatism, Unionism and the Problem of Territorial Management" in Peter Madgwick and Richard Rose, *The Territorial Dimension in United Kingdom Politics*, Macmillan, London, 1982, pp. 149–54.

[35] Dicey and R. S. Rait, *Thoughts on the Union between England and Scotland*, Macmillan, London, 1920, pp. 319ff.

[36] Cf. Ian Hutchinson, *A Political History of Scotland, 1882–1924*, John Donald, Edinburgh, 1986, esp. Ch. 5.

[37] J. S. Gibson, *The Thistle and the Crown*, HMSO, Edinburgh, 1985, pp. 42, 66–72; and see C. T. Harvie, *No Gods and Precious Few Heroes: Scotland since 1914*, Arnold, London, 1987, Ch. 4.

tatives in local government. This principle was continued in Tom Johnston's Council on Industry of 1942, in the Scottish Council: Development and Industry of 1946, and the Scottish Economic Conference, 1948–50. After something of a hiatus, the Macmillan government resumed it in its economic initiatives (the Toothill Committee, and the Central Scotland Plan) of 1960–63.[38]

The second principle was that the Secretary of State could assume that his party and its policy represented and would satisfy a majority of Scots (or near enough a majority as to make no difference). Only very briefly was there a pre-war Secretary of State whose party represented a small minority of the electorate (Sir Archibald Sinclair, Liberal, 1931–2). Tom Johnston, Labour, 1941–45, whose party had gained in 1935 only 20 MPs (but 41.8% of the vote) was very careful to propose action only with the consent of his predominantly Conservative "Council of State" (i.e. of ex-Secretaries). Labour had 49.4% of the votes and 39 MPs, 1945–50, and 46.2% and 37 MPs, 1950–1, and the Unionists 48.6% and 35 MPs, 1951–5, 50.1% and 36 MPs, 1955–59. The Unionist vote fell to 47.2% and 31 MPs, 1959–64 but, as previously observed, Macmillan went to great lengths to secure Labour movement support for his economic policies.[39]

The successful Secretary of State *could* also operate from a secure and influential base within the governing party, but most Unionist Secretaries were members of powerful landed or industrial families, from Collins the publishers to Youngers the brewers. However, after 1959, as Scottish industrial autonomy declined and agricultural policy shifted to the EEC, the anti-Conservative vote also rose, and more than halved the number of Conservative MPs over the next quarter-century.. Unionist Secretaries steadily lost their freedom of action.[40]

Labour Secretaries had different problems. Few matched Tom Johnston, as Scotland was lukewarm about Labour's centralised planning, and although Willie Ross, after 1964, could deliver forty-plus pretty docile backbench votes, he was soon faced with a new competitor, the Welsh Office, a rival whose existence made it difficult for him to claim anything as a success, for fear of stimulating demands for equal treatment from a politician who was—at least geographically— well placed to make them. Matters did not improve after 1972, with the imposition of direct rule on Northern Ireland. The territorial ministers

[38] C. T. Harvie, "Coping with the Slump in Scotland, 1929–1939", delivered at the Scottish Office Centenary Colloquium, Edinburgh 1985, publication forthcoming. See also James Kellas, *The Scottish Political System*, Cambridge 1986, pp. 193–5.

[39] Harold Macmillan, *At the End of the Day, Memoirs, 1961–63*, Macmillan, London, 1973, pp. 393, 403–4.

[40] C. T. Harvie, *No Gods . . . .*, p. 116; Interview, C. T. Harvie with Sir Douglas Haddow (former Permanent Secretary, Scottish Office), 29 Oct. 1986. James Stuart, 1951–57, had been Churchill's Chief Whip.

had expanded, but only to the extent of becoming the weakest and most fissiparous grouping in the Cabinet.[41]

Two further factors intervened: the growth of support to third parties which backed home rule, if not something stronger, and the emergence of Scottish voting patterns which diverged completely from the British norm. The first emerged after 1967 as a reflex of the failure of social democratic planning to supply the welfare goods it posited as "rights". The insecure response of the traditional parties aggravated this. The Wilson government swithered between welfare goals and a different, more "participatory" (and thus perhaps cheaper) definition of rights, and ended by adopting the delaying strategy of a Royal Commission (something offering low risks at the beginning but high risks at the end). The Unionists took the even more irresponsible course of proposing a Scottish Assembly outright. Whatever their fortunes, both parties were doubtless relieved when in 1970 politics reverted to two-party type.[42]

When the crisis announced its return in 1974, this time with the Kilbrandon Commission to back it up, Labour opted (without much conviction) for devolution and participatory rights, only to have these assaulted by the remaining believers in welfare rights. The Conservatives, however, seeing their chance of controlling a Scottish assembly dwindle to zero with the collapse of both their vote and the remaining outposts of a distinctive Scottish capitalism, opted for the paradoxical objective of a traditional "British" national identity coupled with a depoliticisation of society in favour of market choice.[43] The first appeal, at best problematic, succeeded (almost wholly by chance—an Exocet in the wrong place would have finished it) but, as expressed in the elections of 1983 and 1987, only endorsed an "English" idea of Britain. The second, ultimately, promises to be far more corrosive.

State and Market

The result of Thatcherism and the political simplicities which escort it has been a relapse to the formulae of Benthamism (or at least Dicey's elementary version of it). Sanguine Conservatives have seen the "self-righting" operations of the market taking over the political activity implied by planning; in fact what separates their project from the Fascist or Nazi radical right is their Benthamite/Cobdenite commitment to international trade. This "internationalisation" of traditional state structures, however, implies a further subversion of the Benthamite calculus. If one cannot agree on the dimensions of a political unit, how can one calculate whether a group has been so consistently disadvantaged

[41] Interview, John Milne with John S. Gibson, CB, 3 November 1986.

[42] Keith Webb, *The Growth of Nationalism in Scotland*, Penguin, Harmondsworth, 1978, p. 169.

[43] Martin Holmes and Christopher Harvie, *Britain Today: Politics and Social Conditions*, Deutsches Institut für Fernstudien, Tübingen, 1985, pp. 22–31.

by political decisions, to the point where it ceases to be part of the political community? Although Dicey's "period of individualism" involved an uncomplicated economy in which planning by private as well as public bodies was practically unknown, and which tolerated enormous social and civil inequalities, the repeated catastrophes which befell civil society—epidemics, industrial disasters, riots, etc.—could only be settled through public intervention. Aneurin Bevan didn't exaggerate when he wrote that the modern state owed more to the medical officer of health and the sanitary inspector than to the politician.[44] (An analogous issue is the environmental cost of modern economic development, something which can only be coped with through public control. Yet while the boundaries of the appropriate— and necessarily international—units remain uncertain, this critical constraint on the market can be, and in Britain is, disregarded as a political factor.)

The indeterminacy accounts for the elimination of Crosland's "domesticated capitalism". In developed countries over the last twenty years a trend to the political right, evidenced either in votes for Conservative parties, or in the adoption by nominally radical parties of conservative programmes, has stemmed from the weakening hold of the idea of political community, something only enhanced by the evidence of worsening conditions among a minority of their own inhabitants, and among the majority of the world's peoples. This is less in evidence where the institutions of the state—even if decentralised—have consensual support. Scandinavian social democracy, after a dark night of the soul in the 1970s, has proved relatively resilient because an electorate, particularly well-educated in the costs and benefits of the welfare state, thought the matter through and accepted the disciplines implied by high taxation. In Britain, the reaction to the difficulties of such "planning" (not wholly spontaneous but owing much to the positive propaganda of American conservatism) has been to excise the dependent classes—the elderly, the unemployed, racial minorities— from the notional political community and readjust the criteria of political morality to sanction this.

So sustained has been the assault on state provision (though not state coercion) since Bevan's time that it seems almost surprising to maintain that such "welfare" rights as access to pure water and food, sanitary housing, and adequate education are a necessary component of our citizenship. Yet in Britain all "rights" *are* equal, insofar as none have been selected to form the substance of a "Bill of Rights". So welfare rights remain potentially more significant than political conventions, in that they are backed by statute. The Conservative government could throw its power against the conventions: throttling municipal autonomy by cutting grants and capping rates, abolishing the autonomy of the

[44] *In Place of Fear*, Heinemann, London, 1952, p. 98.

BBC, and closing a few universities down. It could transfer the Scottish Office to Whitehall and put English ministers at its head by executive action. But drastic interference with the welfare state has raised much more controversy, as the response to the threat to the National Health Service and the imminence of the Poll Tax now indicates.

The difference from 1886 is that the Scots or the Irish are no longer faced with a monolithic, confident English state, but with a flagging national economy perilously linked to an international exploitative and speculative system. The Conservative assault is not only weakening the bundle of emotions, institutions and concrete benefits to which the establishment has always appealed; it seems to be converting some of these—the Church, the Monarchy—into symbols of resistance. The significance is not how effective this resistance is, but that it is coming from the glue of the constitutional system itself. The self-confident "City ethos" of modern Conservatism is technologically sophisticated but ideologically crude, capable of attracting the financial entrepreneurs of the developed countries and a few parasitic litterateurs, but creating a growing hostility not only from politicians in the declining primary producer countries whose commodities it speculates in, but from the newly industrialised countries themselves. The revolt of the British periphery and large sections of the official intelligentsia confirms that the political factors which have allowed power to be so concentrated are also inherently unstable.

But as the Conservatives, following the radical right typology, become less of a party and more of a regime, their purposive goals also become less predictable. The abandonment of the party's principal strategic convention, which Bulpitt mourns, of much government direction over the economy, and indeed of the principle of Cabinet government, has already led to inconsistent policy gyrations, and will lead to more. However welcome its intent, the Anglo–Irish Agreement is a major example, since the status of Northern Ireland is largely due to Conservative attempts (warmly endorsed by Dicey!) to wreck any agreed federal solution for United Kingdom politics before World War I.[45] The Agreement punches such a huge hole in parliamentary sovereignty that the issue must be raised: will pressure from Scotland act on pragmatism to obtain Scottish home rule?

Although government spokesmen repeatedly denied that any real demand for it existed, home rule was a major issue in Scotland in the 1987 general election, and probably did much to account for the collapse of the Conservatives even in areas like Edinburgh whose economic situation was closer to that of the affluent south-east than to the Ancient Britain archetype of "council housing plus declining heavy industry".

[45] Kendle, "The Round Table|Movement and 'Home Rule all Round'", in *The Historical Journal*, xi 2 (1968), pp. 332–53; and see Richard Rose, "Is the United Kingdom a State?" in Rose and Madgwick, coll. cit.

Labour made devolution the basis of most of its planning and social welfare policies for Scotland, and the vociferous opposition of 1979 either announced itself converted (like Robin Cook MP and Councillor Eric Milligan, now Convener of the Convention of Scottish Local Authorities) or fell tactfully—in the case of Tam Dalyell, unwontedly— silent. A number of Labour unionists had earlier left the party for the SDP, only to be interned within its commitment to devolution.

The result certainly removed some potentially awkward problems. Had there been a Labour government, the devolution commitment might have been jeopardised by a proportionately larger number of English Labour MPs doubtful both about devolution and the likelihood of Scotland continuing to send 72 MPs to Westminster. Had the Alliance held the balance, Labour's preference for using the first-past-the-post system for the Assembly elections would have been a bone of contention. Commitment could still have been dissipated in the intrigues of Westminster, and participatory rights would have featured ambiguously: English voters being comparatively disadvantaged by the privileges granted the Scots; third party voters being disadvantaged by an inequitable voting system. But the outcome reinforced the Scots' contention that their participatory rights were being infringed both by the sovereignty of a party which captured only 24% of the Scottish vote and 10 out of 72 seats, and by the decline and fall of "welfare-based" political and administrative conventions.

Throughout 1988 continual appeals were made for civil disobedience: an unprecedented situation in Scotland. The Labour Party has urged its voters to impede the collection of individuals' poll-tax data; the Scottish National Party has drawn up plans for a mass non-payment campaign by 100,000 sympathisers; the Scottish Committee against the Poll Tax has called on 100 prominent Scots to resist. At the same time Labour MPs are setting up a Select Committee on Scottish Affairs unauthorised by Parliament, and the Campaign for a Scottish Assembly's Constitutional Committee, with an authoritative membership, has created an elected (but again unauthorised) Constitutional Convention. Meanwhile the Conservative vote at the district council elections in May 1988 dropped to 19%.

A further proposal, still in its infancy, urges that approaches be made to an international tribunal, and sympathetic nations, on the grounds that the rights of the Scottish people are being systematically violated by the actions of government. A group of SNP provenance, "Scotland–UN", approached the United Nations Commission on Human Rights on the grounds that the result of the Referendum of 1 March 1979 would have been accepted as a definite expression of opinion under international law. The fact that a majority of Scottish MPs voted for the 40% "Yes" provision in the Scotland Act was countered by the majority of Scots MPs which also voted for the Act to be kept on the Statute Book even after the 40% hurdle was not overcome. To the argument that the

Referendum was about a particular scheme of self-determination, and not the principle in general, the reply must be that the Conservative party—and in particular Lord Home, the chairman of its Committee on Scottish Government in 1968–70—canvassed for a "No" vote, on the grounds that it could produce a better devolution package, a promise which has vanished completely.[46] The grounds for an inter-nation appeal seem tenable, although they would certainly be strengthened if, for example, bodies like the Convention of Scottish Local Authorities were to use the Northern Ireland precedent to demand a referendum on the country's constitutional status and, if necessary, carry it out themselves.

The problem is that the issues which mobilise support—the breach of conventions which are essentially to do with administration and welfare—are not within the purview of, say, the European Convention on Human Rights. The politico-judicial system of the EEC, once assumed to be in the business of promoting the autonomy of regional communities, has been weakened by a reassertion since Britain's accession in 1973 of the privileges of existing nation-states. In terms of their claims to rights of participation, the Scots are trapped between the decay of the conventions of British politics and the unrealised potential of European law: "between two worlds, one dead, one struggling to be born".[47]

Would a case in 1990 wherein Mr Donald Dewar was arrested within the precincts of the Crown Office in the Royal High School of Edinburgh, and charged with trespass in the course of intending to convene an illegal Scottish Assembly, activate Article 14 of the European Convention—deprivation of the rights of a minority? I don't know. But I suspect that, if this happened, the crucial *political* decision would already have been made.

---

[46] *A Claim of Right for Scotland*, Campaign for a Scottish Assembly, July 1988. Home advised voters to "vote No for a better bill", on 14 February 1979 (Bochel, Denver and Macartney, *The Referendum Experience*, Aberdeen University Press, 1981, p. 41). His sinuosity on this issue is remarkable. In 1976 he wrote that "the Scots vote for the SNP because no one has yet given the moderates the measure of control over Scottish affairs which they feel it is reasonable to ask" (*The Way the Wind Blows*, Collins, p. 210) but by 1981 he was attacking the Assembly, and indeed the whole idea of legislative devolution, on the grounds that it was a stepping stone for the SNP.

[47] For the "European Convention of Human Rights" (Council of Europe: 4 November, 1950) see *Europa: Verträge und Gesetze*, Europa Union Verlag 1978, pp. 401–425; see J. Barry Jones, "Wales and Europe" in Osmond, *National Question*, pp. 62–5 and C. T. Harvie, "Europe and the Scottish Nation", Centre for Scottish Economic and Social Research, 1989.

WALKING BACK TO HAPPINESS? CONSERVATIVE PARTY GOVERNMENTS AND ELECTED LOCAL AUTHORITIES IN THE 1980s

JIM BULPITT*

"IN changing the ways in which things have been done for decades, we are predictably accused of attacking local government. I emphatically reject that charge. Certainly local government's powers in certain respects will be limited, but they will be limited in practice not by the Government but by local people. The style of local government will have to become much more 'interactive'."[1]

The subject is central–local relations since 1979. The particular dimension investigated involves the central governments' preoccupations with, and behaviour towards, elected local authorities. The territory examined is Britain. Within Britain, England is granted analytical primacy simply because Scotland and Wales are largely peripheral to the main story, though not necessarily disadvantaged because of that. The principal actor assessed is not some abstract entity called "the Government" or "the Cabinet", but the Conservative Party elite (or leaders) in office. Other parts of the Conservative Party—backbenchers, Central Office and constituency associations—are regarded as mere pressure groups, and not particularly privileged ones at that. The key methodological assumption is that this Conservative elite will behave rationally, or purposefully. Or, to put the point in a weaker form, it is interesting to examine that behaviour *as if* it were rational. Within the British structure of politics that means on most occasions it will pursue a *statecraft* towards local authorities designed, primarily, to protect and promote what it perceives to be its own interests (these perceptions may change over time). It follows that ideology will only be "pulled in" to justify, or add gloss to, behaviour and decisions already determined by statecraft considerations. Hence "Thatcherism", in so far as it purports to be a serious political doctrine, is relegated to the back seat.

---

* Reader in Politics at the University of Warwick. He is the author of *Territory and Power in the United Kingdom*, Manchester U.P., and is currently writing a book on British foreign policy in the 1980s.

[1] Nicholas Ridley, *The Local Right: Enabling not Providing*, Centre for Policy Studies, London, 1988.

This prospectus requires some preliminary comment and amplification.

First, central–local relations in Britain used to rank as one of Oakeshott's subjects of "unimaginable dreariness". It was also of no great party political significance. It may still be dreary, but it is certainly no longer politically unimportant. In the 1980s the subject has been politicised, it has become an issue of (relatively) "high politics" and, in consequence, much of the comment has assumed a highly partisan or essentially contested character. In these circumstances the message is obvious: what follows should be regarded as presenting a case, a point of view, and no more.[2]

Secondly, assessing the main lines of this particular story suffers from the curious inconvenience that the political science of British politics has never developed a coherent formula for analysing the operations of *governments*. It is true that British political science has always expressed an interest in *government*, but the study of particular governments or administrations has been "hived off", with a few exceptions, to "memoir mongers", biographers, journalists and historians. The result, not surprisingly, is that the systematic consideration of British governments hardly exists today as a serious subject.

In an attempt to confront this problem I have developed elsewhere the concept of party elite statecraft, a tool of analysis which influences some of the discussion which follows.[3] Briefly, the principal assumptions which underlie this approach are: (a) that how party leaders in office govern, or manage, the polity is as important as what they do in policy terms; (b) that British party leaders in office possess sufficient relative autonomy from domestic or external forces that they can, if they wish, pursue their own interests (they behave rationally), rather than operate in such a way as to reflect the public interest, or the interests of any particular group or class; (c) that the pursuit of group self-interest can be as crude as the simple desire to avoid trouble or hassle; (d) that in these circumstances, much of what is often regarded as significant in British politics—ideology or policy—is of secondary instrumental importance to these statecraft, politicking, designs; and (e) that in the short and medium run the best operational criterion for assessing the success of governments is that they stay in business, they manage to get re-elected.

These assumptions can be criticised on a number of counts. But they

---

[2] For recent alternative accounts, see: George Jones, "The Crisis in British Central-Local Government Relationships", *Governance* April 1988; Howard Davies, "Local Government Under Siege", *Public Administration*, Spring 1988; R. Rhodes, "Territorial Politics in the United Kingdom" in R. Rhodes and V. Wright (eds), *Tensions in the Territorial Politics of Western Europe*, Frank Cass, London, 1987; and G. Stokes, *The Politics of Local Government*, Macmillan, London, 1988.

[3] See: Jim Bulpitt, "The Discipline of the New Democracy: Mrs Thatcher's Domestic Statecraft", *Political Studies*, 1986; and Jim Bulpitt, "Rational Politicians and Conservative Statecraft in the Open Polity", in P. Byrd (ed), *Foreign Policy Under Thatcher*, Philip Allan, Oxford, 1988.

do help to clarify some of the arguments detailed below. More generally they represent an explicit attempt to tackle that crucial, but neglected, question; namely, how, within the British structure of politics, do we study and assess the operations of particular governments in limited time periods?

Thirdly, in spite of (or, perhaps, because of) this neglect of governments, a large literature on British central–local relations in the 1980s exists. Most of this forms part of an emerging orthodoxy on the subject, an orthodoxy composed of the following themes.

(i) In the 1980s the Thatcher-led Conservative Party governments have pursued a consistent, deliberate, and pernicious policy of centralisation. Local authorities have been reduced to mere administrative agents of the centre.

(ii) The outcome is a radical change in the nature of the British Constitution and/or a radical alteration to traditional methods of state management.

(iii) This is a paradoxical development because, traditionally, the Conservative Party has always supported the values of decentralisation, local democracy and local self-government.

(iv) It is also paradoxical in the comparative sense, because in the 1980s most other Western countries have experienced more decentralisation, more local democracy, and more local self-government.

It is not the task of this paper directly to praise or criticise this orthodoxy. It exists, it should be noted, and its arguments compared with those presented below. This said, the discussion, like the Scottish Football League, is divided into three tenuously connected parts. The first describes the main lines of Conservative policies towards local authorities since 1979; the second considers some conceptual ambiguities present in the study of central–local relations; and the third provides one possible explanation for the developments of the 1980s.

Conservative Leaders and Local Authorities After 1979

What have these Conservative leaders done to elected local governments? One illustrative list of actions runs as follows.

(1) We can start with a matter which, although only indirectly connected with local authorities (and England), is significant in a negative sense. Conservative leaders, and, perhaps above all, Mrs Thatcher, have chosen to ignore the issue of devolution to Scotland and Wales, an issue which played such a malign part in British politics during the 1970s. Of course, this issue is not dead in a party political sense; all the national opposition parties were committed to a devolved Assembly for Scotland at the last election and the Alliance favoured similar institutions for Wales and the English regions. Nevertheless, the Conservatives have pushed this idea off the Government's policy

agenda. Given the events of the 1970s, that represents no mean political achievement.

(2) The traditional system of local authority finance has been radically altered, even swept away. Some examples are as follows.

First, the amount of local authority spending financed by central grants – in aid – has been cut from a national average of about 61% in 1978 to approximately 46% in 1987. For local government this has had tremendously awkward spin-offs in terms of local service standards, consumer satisfaction, and public employee morale.

Secondly, for the first time the central government obtained the right, via the 1980 Local Government, Planning and Land Act and the 1982 Local Government Finance Act, to facilitate the control of *individual* local authority spending by manipulation of their general grant allocation. Subsequently the Rates Act 1984 gave the central government powers to control the amount of revenue raised by individual local authorities from their own rates (rate capping).

Thirdly, the Local Government Finance Act 1988 abolishes domestic rates in England and Wales from 1990. A similar measure for Scotland comes into operation in 1989. Domestic rates will be replaced by a new tax, the community charge or poll tax, which will be levied equally on all adults within each local authority area. There will be rebates for those on low incomes. The Act also allows community charge capping by the central government as a "reserve measure". Rates on business premises will continue to exist, but they will be levied and collected on a uniform national basis by the Government and then distributed to separate local authorities on the basis of a formula to be drawn up by that Government. The upshot is that about 75% of local authority spending will be financed from sources directly controlled by the centre. More generally, a local tax, which dates back to the 16th century, will be abolished by a Conservative Government.

(3) Some existing local authorities have disappeared from the administrative map. The Local Government Act 1985, for example, abolished the GLC and the six metropolitan county councils in England (both established by earlier Conservative governments). The Education Reform Act 1988, as finally constituted, puts an end to the Inner London Education Authority (ILEA). In some cases the functions of these authorities have been transferred to lower tier elected councils. But in many others the services have gone either to central departments, or non-elected quangos, or indirectly elected joint *ad hoc* committees. Whatever their destination, the number of local services managed by directly elected councillors has been reduced.

(4) In the public housing sector, Government policies after 1979 brought about a drastic decline in the number of houses built by local authorities and considerable rent increases for local council tenants. In addition, the Conservatives' "right to buy" policy, which began with the 1980 Housing Act (Tenants Right Act for Scotland in the same year),

enforced the sale of local authority (and other public agency) properties to tenants wishing to buy on highly favourable financial terms. By 1987 it was estimated that over one million tenants had taken advantage of these provisions. Put another way, over one million properties (often the best) had been lost to the public sector. By 1988 the Government was tackling this issue in yet another way: the Housing Act of that year allowed remaining council tenants to "opt out" of local authority control and choose alternative landlords. In short, the Government seemed determined radically to reduce the role of local authorities in the housing sphere. The other side of the coin, the Conservatives' positive commitment to a home-owning democracy, saw an increase in the percentage of owner-occupied households in Britain from 57% in 1979 to 64% in 1988.

(5) Even more radical changes have been pushed through in the field of education. The point can be illustrated if initially the discussion is confined to the six major Education Acts enacted, since 1979, for England.

The first, in 1979, removed the compulsion placed on LEAs by the previous Labour Government to establish fully comprehensive education at the secondary school level. Three others, the Education Acts of 1980, 1981 and 1986, were designed to implement the Conservatives' "Parents' Charter" strategy. They involved: giving parents more choice in the selection of LEA schools; forcing schools to publish more material concerning their activities, staff profiles and academic performances; and expanding the role played by school governors (particularly parent governors) in school management. The 1982 Teachers' Pay and Conditions Act tackled another important subject. It dissolved the Burnham Committee machinery under which, hitherto, LEAs and teacher union representatives had tried to decide questions relating to pay and conditions of service. At the same time the Government imposed not only a new salary settlement but introduced the totally new idea of explicit service contracts for all teachers. The awkward problem of deciding what was to be included in the 1265 hours of "directed time" allocated to individual teachers was devolved onto headteachers.

Finally, in 1988, against considerable opposition, the Conservatives pushed through a comprehensive Education Reform Act. This: gave school parents the right to "opt out" of LEA control in favour of direct funding of the school by the DES; devolved important financial responsibilities, formerly belonging to the LEA, on to school governors and headteachers; imposed a national curriculum and periodic pupil assessment on schools; contained provisions for a network of City Technology Colleges in urban areas, funded by private enterprise and the DES and outside local authority control; and finally, removed polytechnics from the local authority sector. It should also be noted that on some estimates the 1988 Act provided the Secretary of State for Education with some 400 new powers.

This, of course, is mainly the legislative side of the story. It says nothing about the new GCSE examination, the intrusion of the old Manpower Services Commission into matters formerly the sole responsibility of LEAs, the significant increase in the number of parents sending their children to private schools, low teacher morale, prolonged industrial action by some teacher unions, crumbling school buildings, disintegrating textbooks and the advent of computers, accompanied by frantic attempts within schools to justify their appearance.

(6) In many inner city areas Government-nominated agencies and initiatives—Urban Development Corporations, Task Forces and Action Teams—have either reduced, or interfered in, the traditional planning and development functions of local authorities. More generally, until the autumn of 1988, the Department of the Environment (DoE) consistently favoured private development applications against local authority objections at appeal. Mr Ridley's statement to the 1988 Conservative Party Conference that, in 1987, only 2% of 400,000 planning applications were granted centrally on appeal, failed to mention two relevant points. First, most planning applications are unimportant, but a few—those by large private firms—are very important. Secondly, many local authorities have concluded that appeals against big private developments are too dangerous to consider. If a local authority loses an appeal to the DoE, it loses all controls over the infrastructure of the proposed development. Many authorities are not prepared to take this risk.

(7) These Conservative governments have placed restrictions on some aspects of local authority decision-making procedures. For example, the 1986 Local Government Act contained ambiguous provisions banning "party propaganda" financed by rate revenues. Similarly, the 1988 Local Government Act forces local authorities to put many services out to competitive tender and seemingly makes illegal any actions promoting homosexuality. Moreover, in July 1988 the Government's published response to the Widdicombe committee inquiry into local party politics suggested future action banning "twin tracking" by councillors and officials and the employment of political advisors, forcing councillors to reveal their "pecuniary interests", making the exclusion of minority parties from committees illegal, and restricting the expenses claimed by councillors.

(8) Finally, and in more general terms, these Conservative governments, at least since the early 1980s, have engaged in a continuous propaganda war against local authorities, constantly attacking them as undemocratic, inefficient, always prone to overspending, and often the prisoners of extremist, or "loony left", groups. As one local councillor put it: "It's like a Great War artillery bombardment. It goes on and on and on and destroys everything above ground."

Some Problems of Analysis: Concepts Bashing

The main lines of Conservative policies towards local authorities have been described. The exercise highlights both the range and radical nature of the changes involved. It also provides plenty of support for the case that in the 1980s this particular dimension of central–local relations has been centralised, statutised, politicised and Thatcherised.

It would be foolish to deny the force of these arguments. But there are grounds for caution: we should avoid jumping too quickly on to too simple bandwagons. We need to accept, for instance, that in Britain this whole subject is a veritable jungle of conceptual contortions and ambiguities. Three items in this jungle call for some discussion, namely the notions of a unitary state, centralisation and local democracy.[4]

Britain as a Unitary State. It is sometimes argued, especially by lawyers, that the course of central–local relations in Britain since 1979 must be understood as part of the logic of its unitary state. Conservatives, for example, are prone to suggest that the increase in the centre's controls over local authorities is an inevitable consequence of this aspect of the Constitution, whereby legal predominance is granted to Parliament, and through that institution, to the executive. Liberals, on the other hand, while accepting the principle, reverse the message of this argument. They accept that centralisation has increased because Britain is a unitary state, but then damn the unitary principle and support the adoption of federalism, or some "half-way house" between these two principles.[5]

There are several problems here. One is that no academic consensus exists as to the fundamental nature of unitary or federal states, even less any intermediate position. Indeed, only God knows what the unitary principle is, and he has been remarkably reluctant to let mere mortals into the secret. Part of the difficulty is that, in practice, unitary and federal states are structured and operated very differently. Another is that these principles possess multiple dimensions. You can have unitary (and federal) societies, cultures, politics, constitutions and inter-governmental relations. Hence, if we want to say that Britain is a unitary state or polity, we need to specify the particular dimensions on which it scores highly. So far few commentators have bothered to do this. Moreover, even if we accept that the unitary principle has some vague meaning, it is clear that Britain is a very idiosyncratic example: it has an uncodified, highly flexible constitution—in effect, the Constitution is what judges and politicians say it is; and there exists within the English culture deeply embedded support for the notion that Parliament

---

[4] For a more extended treatment of these matters, see Jim Bulpitt, *Territory & Power in the United Kingdom*, Manchester University Press, Manchester, 1983.

[5] Jones, *op. cit.*, provides an alternative argument: the Constitution is unitary, but this only has malign consequences because the system is dominated by the Executive rather than Parliament.

is, or ought to be, sovereign. No other country claiming to be unitary possesses these two characteristics. Thus we can conclude either that talking in terms of the unitary state is an otiose exercise, or that what is significant about Britain goes beyond the unitary principle.

Centralisation. There exists in Britain a diffuse, yet powerful, intellectual consensus that centralisation is a bad thing. Put another way, arguments suggesting the opposite, or even that some caution is required on the matter, are rarely offered or taken seriously in public.

The general foundations of this consensus, however, are woefully weak (though that does not necessarily mean it is "wrong"). Centralisation is usually defined in terms of a central government pinching "local" functions for itself, or possessing considerable powers of control over elected local government. But so little serious academic work has been done on this concept that we are in no position to engage in easy generalisations about its nature and consequences. Put bluntly, since we can't measure centralisation because, at root, we are not certain what it is, we should be cautious about disliking it, or blaming governments for pursuing it. Consider, for example, the following sets of questions.

First, why do we constantly talk of centralisation in general, abstract, terms? Why don't we consider it in relation to the interests of particular individuals or groups in particular locations at particular times? For example, do all Conservative supporters in Haringey, Liverpool or Sheffield necessarily suffer from the centralisation policies of Conservative governments? Likewise, do Labour supporters in Solihull and Wiltshire necessarily suffer from similar policies of Labour governments?

Second, why would any group of rational, national politicians willingly spend much of its time controlling in detail the business of elected local authorities? What benefits do they gain from having to discuss Brent or Liverpool, or the specifics of spending targets and grant penalties, around the Cabinet table or in the Prime Minister's office, or even in the DoE?

Third, why should an attack on the corporate autonomy of local authorities be regarded as an important and dangerous contribution to the creation of a centralised polity?

The point here is that few plausible answers to these questions can be provided from within the confines of the reigning centralisation paradigm. The answers currently on offer come from somewhere else, from a set of associated notions (or ideology) concerning local democracy.

Local Democracy. It is because the British (or, at least, the shouting classes) believe in local democracy that they consider centralisation a bad thing. In other words, centralisation is believed to represent an attack on the things some of the British think they should like.

Why do British intellectuals believe that they and others should value local democracy so highly? The answer is that they have been brought up to accept, or in certain circumstances find it convenient to promote, four propositions: that local democracy is associated with more efficient standards of local service provision than the central government could manage to achieve; that local democracy is nearer to the democratic ideal than national democracy; that local democracy is the essential basis of a national democratic "intelligence"; and that local democracy makes a vital contribution to a pluralist power structure in the polity.

But what is local democracy? To this question, once again the British have developed a coherent and attractive response consisting of several themes: local democracy is representative democracy, that is to say, it is the product of the local electoral process; its ethos is "clean" (i.e. reputable), responsible, public government; its dynamic is located in the workings of elected local authorities; its principal actors are the councillors on those authorities; these local authorities should provide most *local* public services; and, for these various features to be meaningful requires that elected local governments possess significant corporate autonomy from the central government. Thus, for the British, local democracy is local self-public-government, and that is the sum of the corporate activities and freedoms of elected local authorities.

There is no doubt that these are very neat answers to the questions posed. If repeated in parrot-fashion for long enough they assume the status of privileged certainties. But these certainties are sustained more "out of apathy" than serious and constant reconsideration. They do not represent the only answers to these questions and in the late 20th century they may not even be the best answers. Or, if they are the best answers, they are only so because other democratic features of the polity are so minimal. Consider, for example, the following counter points.

Note first the restricted parameters or vision of the British view of local democracy. At anything above the parish level, it is rooted in the twin ideas of representative government and public service (and services) from above. Hence, it makes no attempt to boost citizen participation by the many devices associated with direct democracy, the market, or even political patronage. On this count local democracy is no different from, or better than, national democracy. It also assumes that local interests and the interests of elected local authorities are the same. It is able to do this because local government is not seen to be about majority rule, about minority objections, about politics. The ideal local government process is one based on consensus, on depoliticised (after the elections) communities. Moreover, the notion that local interests (including those of local authorities) may need to be protected and promoted by allowing them a significant displacement *within* the central machinery of government is ruled out. Yet this notion is present in almost all other Western countries and was considered to be important in Britain before the 19th century.

These points inevitably cast some doubt on the advantages local democracy is supposed to generate—advantages which, as presented, are inherently contestable. The strongest argument for a local democracy based on local governments is its contribution to a pluralist power structure in the polity. But, by ignoring the necessity for a capital city presence for local interests and denying the political notion of the local government process, this theoretical advantage is given minimal practical support. Moreover, it is legitimate to question whether, in the late 20th century conditions, this represents the important contribution to pluralism it once did in the 19th century. If it does, it surely says something about the lack of pluralism in other aspects of the polity.

Central–Local Relations in the 1980s: An Explanation

How can we explain the actions of the Thatcher-led Conservative Administrations towards local authorities after 1979? Any such exercise has to accommodate three difficulties: discussions couched wholly in terms of the personalities, policies and ideas of the 1980s are likely to miss much that is relevant to the subject; within the period since 1979 Conservative leaders' preoccupations with local authorities have often changed—this is not a story of plans and policies consistently and coherently pursued; and we cannot easily abstract developments in central–local relations from events in the wider polity. The message then is that explanations are best placed in a macro historical, or developmental, perspective. It is better to be half-right about the whole picture, than half right about a small part of it. A developmental perspective does not mean that once started the process developed a momentum of its own, that it went beyond the control of politicians. It does mean that a radical change of direction demanded more thought and consideration than British politicians have usually seen fit to devote to central–local relations. The implication here is that what the Conservative leaders did between 1982 and 1987 was to take the easiest option open to frustrated politicians. That said, the decade's events can be considered in terms of their historical preconditions and precipitants, and their contemporary triggers and outcomes.[6]

Preconditions. These can be traced back to the statecraft regime which emerged in British politics during the interwar period and persisted, despite policy and personnel changes, through to the early 1960s.[7] The regime was designed to deal with four big problems: the advent of universal adult suffrage, the rise of the Labour Party and Labour movement, the general acceptance that some form of welfare state was required, and the continuing relative decline of British power and the British economy. Baldwin laid the foundation stones of the regime, but it was Neville Chamberlain who supplied and implemented

[6] The terms preconditions, precipitants and triggers are lifted from Lawrence Stone's book *The Causes of the English Revolution, 1529–1642*, RKP, London, 1972.

[7] A regime is a pattern of statecraft which persists over time. For more extended treatment of this period, see Bulpitt, 1983.

the plans for the rest of its structure. Its attractions to politicians in office were such that it survived the Second World War, the Attlee Administration, Keynesians, and the hijacking of the Conservative Party by the Churchill gang in 1940.

Local authorities had a place in this regime, but only a modest one. In effect, its rulers developed the implications, though perhaps not the spirit, of the British vision of local democracy described above. Local authorities were regarded primarily as administrative agencies which existed to implement centrally decided policies. Like children they were expected to be "good", respectable indoors and outdoors, and respectful to the centre. Misbehaviour was frowned upon, but its consequences were conveniently left unclear, because in most instances punishment was in the hands of the judiciary. For the most part, however, the principal operational features of central–local relations during this period ensured that local authorities did not misbehave. These were as follows.

(1) Although British society remained highly localised, exhibiting intense loyalties to some local institutions (for example, professional football teams), such loyalties did not extend to local authorities. Popular culture was either indifferent to, suspicious of, or directly antagonistic towards, elected local government.

(2) This world of local government was a deeply divided one. The divisions and suspicions between city, suburban and rural authorities effectively obstructed the development of a strong, coherent local government "voice" in the polity.

(3) The rates, the major source of locally raised revenues, were both unpopular and divisive within local authorities. They were unpopular with those who paid them, leading to constant pleas for financial retrenchment. In terms of local political cultures they separated legitimate citizens, "the ratepayers", from "the rest". As local public services expanded, especially after 1945, they were financed increasingly by central grants. These conveniently papered over local divisions, yet introduced the potential for greater central control.

(4) The displacement of local interests (including those of local authorities) at Westminster and in Whitehall was low. The national political parties increasingly divorced themselves from local interests, even their own constituency organisations. Leaders and followers met uncomfortably once a year at national conferences.

(5) The central departments, lacking resources in both London and in the field, possessed little detailed knowledge about the activities of most local authorities. Any controls or commands they might wish to exert had to be delivered in general terms. They were not, for example, in a position to control directly the budgets of individual councils.

(6) At the time, however, this did not matter. National party leaders when in office were not interested in the detailed supervision of local government. For Conservative leaders this was *not* because they positively believed in decentralisation, local democracy and local self-

government. Most of them viewed local authorities in the same way as they viewed their constituency associations, at best with indifference, at worst with contempt, and always to be avoided. Real politics took place at Westminster; proper government was the concern of Whitehall. The autonomy Conservative leaders were interested in was their own autonomy *from* local government and local interests.

(7) The result was what can be called a Dual Polity, a structure of central–local relations in which national and local politics, and national and local government, operated, by and large, in two separate compartments. A considerable degree of intergovernmental decentralisation coexisted with a party system and political culture which did not positively favour decentralisation or a vital system of local government.

Overall, it is difficult to label this system centralised or decentralised. With hindsight, however, it is clear that it was potentially very dangerous for local authorities. They possessed little positive citizen support, were divided amongst themselves, were increasingly reliant on central financial handouts, and lacked political muscle where it counted, in Parliament and Whitehall. Ultimately, the survival of the autonomy they possessed rested in the hands of others, in particular the national party leaders and their continual perception that their interests did not require more central control.

Precipitants. The period between the early 1960s and the late 1970s was responsible for this part of the story. Three developments in the wider polity need to be noted: the doctrines of planning or re-modernisation which emerged in the early 1960s; the rise of Welsh and Scottish nationalism in the early 1970s; and the economic and financial crises of the British central state machine, which occurred in the mid-1970s. For central–local relations these threw up three significant debates, two public and one semi-secret. The public debates concerned the reform of local government and various plans for devolution to Scotland and Wales. The semi-secret debate involved the future pattern and control of local authority spending in the context of a newly-perceived general need to curb public expenditure growth.

The devolution debate had no positive institutional outcome. However, it wasted a lot of people's time, enabled Labour to win the 1974 elections, and then, in retribution, ensured its loss of the crucial Parliamentary confidence vote in the Spring of 1979. The reform of local government debate did have positive (though not necessarily beneficial) outcomes: London government was reformed in the 1960s and provincial Britain was subjected to a similar exercise in the early 1970s. Significantly, or amusingly, both reforms were pushed through by Conservative governments. They both created larger, and supposedly more efficient, local authorities. In the process, the national parties extended their colonisation of local councils. In short, these reforms politicised local government from above. What they did not do was to raise citizens' loyalty quotients to their new authorities. How could any one be loyal to, or supportive of, such political and sociological monstrosities as Brent and the West Midlands County Council?

The real implications of the mid-1970s economic crises for central–local relations were neatly avoided by Labour's creation of the Consultative Council on Local Government Finance. This neo-corporatist device was its public response to this particular debate. It gave the appearance of a positive and beneficial strategy whilst delaying serious thought and action on the issue. The Treasury, intelligently pessimistic as always, began to develop (or rehash?) half-secret plans for more stringent and more direct controls over local authority spending. Up to 1979 the Labour government had prudently refused to act on these.

To sum up: during a period when most politicians favoured remodernising Britain, precious little of this managed to penetrate the system of central–local relations. Considerable energy was wasted on debating, and sometimes implementing, institutional reforms. But, in general, this period is important for what did not happen. It produced no viable reform of local government finance, the central government still did not have the right to control the budgets of individual local authorities, and little was done to sort out the growing mess surrounding the local administration of housing, education and planning. On the other hand, it saw no improvement in the displacement of local interests within Westminster and Whitehall. The old Dual Polity was collapsing, but politicians of all parties had ensured, through a mixture of sloth and appeasement, that nothing positive had been put in its place. When the complaints are made about the events of the 1980s, the complainers should not forget these locust years.

Triggers, May 1979–June 1982. The first Thatcher-led administration did not arrive in office determined to clobber local authorities, restrict their traditional freedoms, and establish a more centralised state. But neither was it committed to expanding the role of local authorities in the polity and constructing a more decentralised state. What it wanted from central–local relations was more complex and probably not completely worked out. Hence what it did appeared confusing, was presented confusingly, and was made even more confusing by Labour's inability to comprehend the language employed. The language was new. It did not reflect or support the traditional British banalities of the central–local government "partnership" and the automatic virtues of local authority self-government.

A prime example was the Local Government, Planning and Land Act of 1980, which, with its Block Grant and Grant Related Expenditure Assessments, was attacked by Labour as a centralising statute. It is true that this measure gave the centre the right, for the first time, to attempt to influence the spending decisions of individual local authorities by the threat of manipulating, or cutting, their central grant allocations. But it still left local authorities free to raise the revenues they thought they required from their own rate income, subject, of course, to endorsement at local elections. Here we encounter in practical form the theoretical problems surrounding centralisation discussed above. Put bluntly, why should such provisions be seen as examples of centralisation? There is no higher law which commands that central grants should operate as a vast system of outdoor relief for high-spending local authorities. The central government is responsible for macro-economic management and local spending is an input into that management. Manipulating grants to influence the spending decisions of individual local authorities accepts the obvious: macro-economic management is an aspect of politics and will be pursued according to the political ideas of the party in office. This is what party government is about. The ability to reach down to single local authorities makes grant management both more efficient and fairer. Similarly, and obviously, determining the total amount of grant aid to all local authorities is a party political decision. Central–local relations cannot be run as some protected reserved area where party politics is forbidden.

What the Conservative leadership appeared to want from central–local relations in this initial period was a system of separate, reciprocal autonomies. Each level of government would look after its own as far as possible; but inevitably the centre had a wider responsibility (and mandate). This gave it the right to adjust grants, which qualified the separateness principle in the manner, and for the reasons, just described. In so far as we can generalise about this period, it seems that the Conservatives were attempting to recreate the old Dual Polity. It follows that this initial Conservative strategy was an attempted reconstruction of times past, rather than a revolutionary break from the past.

The strategy, of course, failed. It failed partly because reconstructing the past is a difficult exercise, requiring more serious thought and perseverance than Conservative leaders were prepared to give at the time. But it also failed because in the early 1980s a lethal combination of forces emerged to destroy it. The first was the Government's failure to control inflation and its announced main cause, public expenditure. Local government spending was a more convenient scapegoat for this failure than the centre's own weaknesses on this count. Moreover the Government's gradual realisation that "monetarism was not enough" shifted attention to the supply side of the economy. Once again this put local government in the firing line as a prime obstacle to a more efficient economy. Secondly, the Conservatives painfully learnt that their faith in the ultimate deterrent of the local electoral process on local authorities was misplaced. The interesting attempt to extend that process to include referenda, contained in the first version of what eventually became the Local Government Finance Act 1982, was defeated by a curious combination of Labour MPs and Conservative councillors. Hence the increasing reliance on targets, penalties, the abolition of supplementary rates (in England and Wales) and the appearance of the Audit

Commission. The whole system of financial controls became increasingly complex, bizarre, and ultimately ridiculous in terms of the time, effort and trouble involved. Thirdly, the arrival on the scene of a number of councils controlled by the new Labour Left convinced most Conservatives that they could never again rely on the collaborative capacities of local Labour groups. These developments triggered Mrs Thatcher's direct interest in central–local relations. After the Falklands War, she and her new Chief Secretary to the Treasury, Leon Brittan, hijacked future Conservative policies on these matters. A foretaste of the new strategy was announced by Mr Brittan in June 1982. The message was clear: if local authorities refused to behave on the spending front, then nasty things would happen to them. Few doubted that Mrs Thatcher arnd Mr Brittan would eventually conclude that local authorities had continued to misbehave.

Outcomes. Consider, in statecraft terms, the Conservative leaders' dilemma in the summer of 1982. What could they do about local government, particularly its spending activities? They could not ignore it. Nor could they bargain with it, if only because the Labour Left councils were not open to bargaining: their proclaimed objective was to bring down the Government, not cooperate with it. Moreover, bargaining smelt of Heathism and Labour-style corporatism, things Thatcherism was designed to avoid. This was an administration jealous of its autonomy and authority. Fine-tuning the relationship was also a non-runner, at least in the short term. It is true that the Government now possessed the ability to exert some influence over the spending patterns of individual local authorities. But, as we have seen, capitalising on this influence was a long, slow, arduous, and often embarrassing process. Elsewhere governments could use prefects or political patronage (or both) to clear their path, but these devices were not available in Britain. Ultimately the courts could play a role, but they too were slow and not always reliable.

Remember too that at this stage in the story the Government had concluded that resolving the problems of the British economy was yet another long, slow haul and one largely determined by external forces, particularly that awkward, unpredictable factor of foreign confidence in the pound. Public expenditure control played an important part in determining that confidence. Hence, once again local government trespassed on the Government's economic "space". Moreover, although this was a post-Falklands culture, the Conservatives could not be sure that, with three million unemployed and a putative multi-party system, they would be returned at the next election with a majority. The next manifesto would have to be an anodyne document, but local government (and privatisation) could provide some more positive content. In addition, radical manifesto commitments on local government would bind any future Minister at the DoE, hitherto not a stronghold of Thatcherism.

So in the end there was not much choice. Conservative leaders allowed themselves to be carried by Mrs Thatcher into radical commitments on rate-capping and the abolition of key local authorities. It was the obvious, easy and rational way out of their dilemma. Any other would have taken more serious thought and certainly more time. The outcome was that the second Thatcher Administration was associated with many policies which increased controls over local authorities, examples of which were detailed in the first section of this paper. If the story ends there then the centralisation argument receives considerable support, although more as a tale of muddle and cock-ups than a systematic grand strategy.

But the interesting point is that the story does not stop there. Since the 1987 election, Conservative leaders have begun to articulate yet another centre strategy for local government. This time some serious thought appears to have been applied to the issue and the result is an interesting and, in party political terms, plausible package. In short, like good rational politicians everywhere, the Conservative elite have learnt from past mistakes and built on established positions.

There appear to be a number of specific reasons for this development. One was these leaders' growing distaste for, and embarrassment with, the detailed financial controls over local councils put into place after the early 1980s. A second was the associated felt need to provide a better intellectual gloss on the party's local government policies than simply attacking local authorities. In a sense the Conservatives were looking for something similar to the role played by monetarism in the party's strategy in the mid-1970s. Another reason was the arrival on the ministerial scene from the early summer of 1986 of three politicians who were interested in developing a justificatory ideology for the Government's actions, namely Nicholas Ridley, Kenneth Baker and Douglas Hurd. Finally, the business of pushing through the community charge and education reform measures in 1988 gave both Ridley and Baker the chance to systematise their thoughts on these matters. A convenient way into this new strategy is to consider the pamphlet published by Ridley on local authorities in February 1988, a document which (if taken seriously) must rank as one of the most interesting discussions of the subject produced by a serving minister in the 20th century.[8]

Ridley's principal themes, if I understand him correctly, run as follows.

(1) The Conservatives have now established a statutory framework which, at one and the same time, allows local authorities to operate effectively and prudently within the the national polity and ensures that the central government has some chance of controlling their activities. Hence, it is now time for attention to switch from the macro to the supply side of this particular piece of political economy.

[8] Ridley *op. cit.* See also N. Hepworth, "What future for Local Government?", IEA, London, 1988.

(2) Individual citizens as consumers, and not local authorities, should be regarded as the major political actors in local democracy. Citizen-consumers are concerned, above all, with the efficient and economical provision of local services. They are not too bothered about who or what provides those services.

(3) It follows that there is no reason why local councils should be all-purpose, monopoly suppliers of local services. The market place and competition may be more effective mechanisms of goods and services supply. What matters is that these products are provided in economical and responsive ways. If, then, service to the consumer is the prime task of local authorities, councils must decide which services they can best provide themselves, which are best produced by private agencies, and which require some combination of the two.

(4) Thus the roles of local councils and councillors should change from universal providers and service managers to those of enablers and deciders of priorities—deciding which agencies should be "enabled" to provide local services. Two incidental advantages of these new roles will be to reduce the power of local government unions and free local officials from undue party political pressures.

(5) This means that local councillors, especially Conservative ones, should assume a more "politicised" strategic role in local affairs than hitherto. Deciding who will be enabled to provide local services is the proper role of politics in local government. At the same time it will ensure that Conservative councillors will be of more direct assistance to Conservative leaders at the centre.

(6) In these various ways, the very necessary political accountability of local governors to their electors will be increased. The task of controlling local councils will rest where it should be—with local citizens, not the central government. Achieving this goal will be enormously assisted by the community charge legislation. This will not only remove the Government from continuous detailed supervision of local finances but will force all local adult residents to become more active citizens in the local political process. As a by-product it will abolish that awkward cultural division between the ratepayers as legitimate local citizens and the rest as non-legitimate ones.

What can be said about this new strategy? In some senses it is merely a more coherent version (in an improved climate) of what Michael Heseltine and Tom King were trying to put over in the early 1980s. But it goes further than that, and further than the negative, carping, centralism of the second Thatcher Administration. For the first time there is a clear and direct connection between what the Conservatives want from national politics and their views on central–local relations and the role of local authorities. The strategy looks radical and Ridley, for one, believes it is radical—a decisive break with the past. But politicians do not necessarily understand the full implications of what they do, or want to do. Ridley's propositions depend on which past he is referring to. Certainly the new strategy is a break with the 1960s and 1970s. But, perhaps, the ghost of Alderman Alfred Roberts of Grantham would not be too surprised at its messages; for in many ways what we have here is a counter-revolutionary vision and strategy (and not to be damned because of that). This is another attempt to get central–local relations back to the 1930s, when the two levels of government knew their respective places. Local government becomes, once again, limited government—respectable and prudent within its own confines and respectful to the central government. Neville Chamberlain (and the Treasury View) would have liked this particular tune. We should not be surprised at this development. After all, it merely reflects the more general counter-revolutionary vision of the various Thatcherite projects since 1979.

Conclusions

Conclusions are difficult because the subject is both contentious and more complex than commonly supposed. If we had referees, every account of British central–local relations in the 1980s would be given, at the outset, a yellow card. Many will regard the case presented here as too favourable an account of the Conservative leaders' operations. That may be so. It is worth pointing out though that as a "country" member of the Conservative Party I have found many of the policies followed either disturbing, or farcical, or both. But personal opinions and party affiliations are not relevant here. It is not the task of academics to change the world, but to explain it, warts and all, even if we do not like it. The simple orthodoxy that the Conservative leaders have become bloody-minded centralisers deserves to be turned over from time to time, not only as poor description but as an argument based on contested concepts and suspect elite psychology. What this exercise has done is to raise some awkward questions about the subject. They are worth repeating. How do we study or assess party governments operating over limited time periods? How do we best promote or defend local interests? Are local authorities and councillors necessarily the principal actors of local democracy? What is a centralised polity?

This article has provided one approach to the first question. Conservative leaders have provided their own answers to the others. They may not be "nice" answers; they may not be sustained in the future; but they were the answers manufactured by one set of politicians in office during a world recession, in a highly open economy, and with, at the beginning, precious few instruments effectively to control, or even influence, many local authorities. Whatever we conclude about this experience it is clear that the Conservative elite have jettisoned much of the cant and casuistry traditionally employed to describe the British territorial constitution. On those grounds alone they deserve some credit.

PART II
THE EUROPEAN EXPERIENCE

BRITISH DOGMATISM AND FRENCH PRAGMATISM REVISITED

DOUGLAS E. ASHFORD*

LOCAL government has never occupied an important place in the minds and hearts of British leaders. In 1886 Lord Salisbury wrote to Randolph Churchill, "I wish there was no such thing as local government."[1] Gladstone was even less impressed by the municipally financed splendours of Birmingham than he was by Chamberlain's radical republicanism. Neither leader found Sir George Goschen's demonstration of the fiscal impotence of Victorian cities very compelling. These historical footnotes raise the question of whether the priorities given local government have really changed over the past century. High-handed fiscal and financial controls, crudely manipulated local boundaries and unbelievably corrupt local elections are all part of the British political tradition. In a curious extension of monarchal absolutism, Prime Ministers have long considered local government their playground.

If Star Chamber justice for local government is nothing new, the interesting question becomes why the major parties have done nothing to attach political esteem and influence to local authorities over the past century. The simple answer is of course that, unlike politicians in every other democracy, British leaders do not need local support in order to enjoy the power and prestige of national office. Though sadly deteriorated in recent years, national electoral organizations have not depended on local party organization for local finance, while local election procedures, as the Widdicombe Report has finally confessed, are so intricate that few understand what happens in local elections. For decades Whitehall has successfully concealed the fact that without the hardworking local civil service of British towns and counties, government policies would grind to a halt. A few years ago inviting four local civil servants to spend a year in Whitehall was regarded as a major administrative innovation. An audible sigh of relief swept Parliament in

* Douglas E. Ashford is Andrew W. Mellon Professor of Comparative Politics at the University of Pittsburgh. His numerous publications on local government in Britain and France include *British Dogmatism and French Pragmatism: Center-Local Relations in the Welfare State*, 1982. His most recent book is *The Emergence of the Welfare States*, Oxford and New York, Blackwell, 1986.
[1] Quoted in J. P. D. Dunbabin, "V. The Politics of the Establishment of County Councils", *Historical Journal*, v. 6, 1963, p. 226.

1976 when the Labour Government trashed fifty years of debate and study of how Britain might benefit from regional government.

Compared to the governments of continental Europe and North America, the British have erected virtually impenetrable barriers between national and local government. More surprising yet, the ramparts are carefully guarded on both sides. Local politicians are often thought of as party hacks or party regulars, viewed with equal suspicion by local and national bureaucrats. Local civil servants have improved their image of late, but still conform to the rigid compartmentalization Whitehall imposes and in some cases—education perhaps—have so long enjoyed a symbiotic tie to their national-level peers that innovative decision-making is almost impossible. Even the term "intergovernmental politics" is rarely heard in British political debate. The sort of territorial collusion of the French *grands corps* to monopolize important new programmes holds few attractions for Whitehall mandarins. Though half or more of British MPs have held local government office, the Westminster model is replete with disincentives to encourage them to draw on their experience. As one dedicated to dismantling government, Mrs Thatcher could not be expected to take seriously the growing interdependence of territory and function, but then neither did a long line of Prime Ministers who preceded her.

The result has been that local government has always been politically vulnerable in Britain (perhaps less so in Scotland). It never acquired the revolutionary legitimacy of the French commune, or even the tradition of political progressiveness of the ancient German trading cities. Even in highly centralized Sweden, the concentration of local amenities and services in the local "folk house" catches the imagery of communal social democracy. American cities carved out their historical niche at the turn of the century as the vehicle of the municipal reform movement and at mid-century by becoming the focus for the racial integration of America. Insularity in British policy-making means that the flexibility which intergovernmental adjustment brings to complex political and social questions is denied Parliament as well as local councils. A recent example of the British simplification is Widdicombe's characterization of New York City as a typical strong-mayor type of urban government.[2] Even mayors less dependent on rhetoric than Mayor Koch would agree that most of their time is spent racing from one autonomous board meeting to another in hopes of getting a grip on their own city. To be the political leader of a German *Land*, an Italian region or an American state is a political job *par excellence* and is known as such in assigning political rewards, prestige, and opportunities.

The historical handicap of British local government has never been fully appreciated by British politicians and policy-makers. More accurately perhaps, the ease of subordination has never seemed strange.

[2] Report of the Committee of Inquiry into the Conduct of Local Authority Business, *The Conduct of Local Government Business*, London, HMSO, June 1986, Cmnd 9797.

BRITISH DOGMATISM AND FRENCH PRAGMATISM

In eighteenth century England the conversion of local patronage to parliamentary necessities was the bedrock of early cabinet government. Plumb wrote, "If the Lord Lieutenancy was the loom upon which the pattern of local patronage was woven, the justices of peace were its restless shuttles".[3] Squashing the Speenhamland decision to provide adequate outdoor poor relief in 1795 was only the first of dozens of national decisions reducing local government to fiscal impotence and eliminating local discretion. The painful process of reforming Parliament and enlarging the electorate during the nineteenth century meant that local government reform was always a secondary concern. The aristocracy protected their rural strongholds until the Local Government Act of 1888 finally abolished the justices of the peace as the county governors. The radical reformers had hardly more respect for local sensitivities or local democracy. Sir Edwin Chadwick, like Sidney Webb a century later, saw local inefficiencies and waste as an obstacle to good government. Lord Redcliffe-Maud (then Sir John Maud) translated the Fabian message into "accountability" in the 1960s, but the message was the same: local government is ineffective, unreliable and disorganized.

The unrelieved monotony of centre-local relations in Britain may be more apparent to the foreign observer than to the local practitioners.[4] Local democracy receives obligatory nods of approval but it has never been imagined as integral to democratic government, and history never presented the British people with a situation where its value as a reservoir of democratic faith might be demonstrated. Local services were always imagined as a complement to national designs and needs. While the level of services varies among local authorities as much in most democracies, a myth overcame Whitehall that the "locals" were a threat to orderly policy-making. In a system where fiscal and financial control is the keystone to parliamentary supremacy, it is perhaps less surprising that local resources and local taxation have always been regarded with a jaundiced eye by Chancellors of the Exchequer and their mandarins. Taking a closer look at these three potential foundations for politically autonomous local government may show how Mrs Thatcher's excesses are actually in the mainstream of British centre-local relations. She has only taken to a logical extreme what many before her often did.

---

[3] J. H. Plumb, "Robert Walpole's World: The Structure of the Government", in D. Baugh, ed., *Aristocratic Government and Society in 18th Century England*, New York, New Viewpoints, 1975, p. 123.

[4] Douglas E. Ashford, *British Dogmatism and French Pragmatism: Center–Local Relations in the Welfare State*, London and New York, Allen & Unwin, 1982. While many of the ninteenth century French liberals admired the British parliament, such persons as Tocqueville, Boutmy (the founder of the Ecole Libre de Science Politique) and Halévy agreed that British local affairs were poorly organized for a democratic state.

THE NEW CENTRALISM

Local Democracy: Why Bother?

Although one can understand Mrs Thatcher's frustration with the London boroughs that held courses on nuclear protest and gay liberation, the eradication of the Greater London Council is an act of political extremism that would be unimaginable in any other democracy. Though less embarrassing, one can compare the dissolution of London's government with Mitterrand's tolerance of his arch rival and until recently his own Prime Minister as mayor of Paris. Chirac not only used the Hôtel de Ville to organize a virtual counter-government but held his own Armistice Day parades and diplomatic receptions. In the rough and tumble of American local politics, political incongruities abound, not the least being the state of New York whose governor acts like the mayor of New York City while the mayor barely conceals his conviction that he should be governor. In most democracies, local politics add vigour and interest to democratic life; not so in Britain. The effect is that local governments have little political capital with which to defend themselves when radical reformers make them redundant.

Trevelyan noted that municipal reform depended on parliamentary reform[5] and therein lies the secret to the political subordination of local democracy. The reform of parliamentary boroughs had to precede municipal reform. Even so, when the Reform Bill of 1832 created 143 new seats in the Commons, only 65 went to the virtually unrepresented cities and towns. Sixty-nine small parliamentary boroughs still had a total population of only 390,000 persons.[6] Ignoring Peel's advice that municipal reform follow without stiff opposition, the Tory lords insisted that a quarter of the elected councils under the Municipal Reform Act of 1835 be elected for life. Only 178 of the 285 towns and cities studied by the Royal Commission on Municipal Corporations were given elected councils and, of course, the counties kept the patronage system. There were fewer persons enfranchised by the 1835 Act than by the 1832 Reform Bill.[7] Local democracy has never held much charm for British leaders.

It can hardly be said that Britain rushed into democratic government during the nineteenth century, and local government necessarily brought up the rear. The Local Government Act of 1888, with its subsequent laws on rural and urban districts, is generally considered the milestone in advancing local democracy. It was in fact carefully drawn to ensure the separation of town and country. Rutland's 21,000 inhabitants were given the same government as Lancashire's 3.5 million. Towns of

[5] Sir Charles Trevelyan, *British History of the Nineteenth Century*, London, Longman, 1937, p. 244.

[6] Joseph Redlich and Francis W. Hirst, *Local Government in England*, London, Macmillan, 1903, v. 1, p. 81.

[7] Bryan Keith-Lucas, *The English Local Government Franchise*, Oxford, Blackwell, 1952, pp. 59–64.

over 50,000 were excluded from county government (the government had actually favoured a more generous figure of 150,000) to insulate pastoral virtues from urban vices. The Local Government Board, an ineffective agency, carefully ignored the clause calling for local financial reform, and the London vestry system helped preserve Tory London government until the 1934 election. Britain was hardly rushing headlong into local democracy, nor did anyone in Westminster seem to care that it was not. The enthusiastic urban reformer, Joseph Chamberlain, quickly abandoned his local concerns when more promising political paths opened up within the Tory party. A long list might be made of MPs both before and after this time who quickly learned that Westminster democracy has little to do with local democracy.

One of the neglected questions of local government studies in Britain is whether local political forces could be mobilized even if there was the will to do so. There are clearly a number of circumstances that make this unlikely. Although parties regularly intervene in local council proceedings through caucus rule, the party organization rarely depends on local council organisation for electoral purposes. The main reason is that through a series of flukes only about a third of the parliamentary constituencies conform to local government boundaries. Part of the reason is that national politicians have felt free to fiddle with the presumably statutory imposition of parliamentary redistricting, the most serious case perhaps being Callaghan's delay in 1969 in hopes of guarding about 20 Labour seats.[8] A winner-take-all national electoral system means that considerations of local democracy have little weight when parliamentary survival is at stake. Much the same fate awaited the Royal Commission on the Constitution and regional government. Few realized that at almost the same moment when parliamentary convenience in Britain condemned a minor effort to invigorate local democracy, an overbearing and proud President of France was driven from office by a regional referendum that most French citizens felt was manipulative.

For all the sociological poring over the sad fate of British local democracy, local voting and party behaviour may be no more than an accurate reading by British citizens of their relative impotence in the governing process. Turnout in British local elections is about 40 per cent compared with 70 per cent in France, 85 per cent in Italy and a whopping 90 per cent in Sweden.[9] In solid Labour cities it can fall to 25 per cent of the voters. It was, of course, the erosion of local democracy that inspired the Militant Tendency to take over local councils on their way to taking over the Labour Party. Though obviously no reason for Mrs Thatcher to show mercy in demolishing local democratic rule, it was Labour Party neglect of local government and reliance on labour union barons to control the party conference that left the

[8] According to David Butler and Michael Pinto-Duschinsky, *The British General Election of 1970*, London and New York, Macmillan, 1971, pp. 414–415.
[9] *The Conduct of Local Business*, p. 38.

Militant Tendency free to seize power at the grassroots. Whether Thatcher or the Trotskyites have more seriously abused local democracy is an open question; it just happens that Mrs Thatcher is Prime Minister.

Participation has never been a French problem. Elections for factory councils (*comités d'entreprise*), working condition committes (*prud'hommes*), social security councils and local government councils abound in France. Indeed, the French become weary with the heavy electoral demands placed on them. The Socialists were determined to take this trend a step further. There are now elected councils replacing the once co-opted regional committees. Departmental councils now have their own staff and services (some promptly hired their previous national officials) and communes will also be free to enlarge their staffs as they choose. Contrary to the image of an over-centralized France, each departmental council was free to work out its own procedure for the transfer of staff, facilities and budgets. French local elections are much simpler than British local elections but they have never been simply a bell-wether of national elections. Local elections are a proving ground for new political coalitions, including the Common Programme that helped bring the Socialists to power in 1981.[10] There are many signs that the right is now using the decentralized power of the *loi Defferre* to enhance its own sagging image. Though certainly no Ken Livingstone, Chirac was free to use his position as mayor of Paris to harass Mitterrand.

Mrs Thatcher's extremism may have inadvertently revived concern for local democracy in Britain. Even Neil Kinnock can no longer assume that local councils will echo national party leaders. For many years there were elaborate efforts to make local government non-partisan. The history of the local government associations is largely that of a father and son operation which arranged private member bills to meet local needs rather than have local governments directly lobbying through party channels.[11] Parliamentary indifference arose because local politics was taken out of political hands. Oddly enough, for many years local authorities seemed to find political impotence reassuring. As late as 1965 two-thirds of the local councillors thought party politics an impediment to conducting local business. According to the Widdicombe survey, a decade later all the negative attitudes have hardened. The caucus system still conceals decision-making from voters and reduces the opposition, as in Westminster, to an irritant in the policy process. Mrs Thatcher and the Militant Tendency have conspired to politicize local councils but to no useful purpose. Of course the label "independent" was often an honourable evasion of political responsibility for local Tory patriarchs, especially in rural areas. All this helped preserve the illusion that local policy-making is politically neutral and in so doing helped play into the hands of those who suspected that local government was

[10] See Ashford, *British Dogmatism and French Pragmatism*, pp. 147–154.
[11] See Bryan Keith-Lucas and Peter Richards, *A History of Local Government in the Twentieth Century*, London and New York, Allen and Unwin, 1978, pp. 180–198.

naturally inefficient and wasteful, a view commonly expressed in Westminster since Bentham, Chadwick and Simon battled against the locals a century ago.

Local Services: For Whose Needs?

An interesting argument can be made that the political neutralization of local democracy served Westminster in the same way that administrative neutralization of local government served Whitehall. Just as the British higher Civil Service acquired ministerial support by insulating ministers from the conflicts and tedium of Whitehall, so also the local government service insulated Whitehall from the complexities of policy implementation. Crossman is only the most frank of ministers who found it convenient to blame local inadequacies for scandals and errors that in any other democratic system would more squarely fall on political shoulders. Indeed, there is a certain irony in the fact that he unleashed the two reports that confirmed central fears that local government was letting the nation down. A tough-minded Thatcher needed little tutoring to grasp the convenience of this argument in whittling local government down to radical Tory dimensions. Even a lesser political animal could not have failed to see how the public sector unions destroyed the Callaghan government. The ritual of self-destruction began before Thatcher arrived in office.

Administrative neutrality and administrative complacency have Victorian roots. Though no longer workable, the late nineteenth century practice of correcting the Whitehall copybook with private member bills was a convenient way to conceal the inadequacy of national statutes governing local affairs. Allowing MPs to ignore party lines in order to obtain privileges for individual local authorities was a way of preserving the consensual pretence essential to parliamentary supremacy without having to deal with messy intergovernmental questions. No doubt influential local civil servants could thump on Whitehall desks. Harassed mandarins were often prepared to overlook local divergencies, but the political significance of an intricate system of mutual adjustment was for the most part carefully concealed by mutual consent.

Policy-making at the national level is well devised to perpetuate the hoax. The curious question is why local governments allowed themselves to be so regularly blamed by Westminster and Whitehall for shortcomings and errors that in any other democracy would be regarded a national disgrace. The tradition was well developed from the early nineteenth century. In his Poor Law report, Sir Edwin Chadwick delighted in pointing out how a Derby school had only one pupil and Bath had four police forces. A more diplomatic man, Sir John Simon, battled Whitehall and a corrupt London government for a decade before withdrawing from local administration.[12] Edwardian giants of Whitehall

[12] Royston Lambert, *Sir John Simon, 1816–1904, and English Social Administration*, London, MacGibbon and Kee, 1963.

such as Sir John Morant could barely conceal their disapproval of local government. What seems strange to an external observer is that the internal conflicts and deadlocks of Whitehall servants over local issues were so seldom aired and that the local officials labouring under this handicap were so compliant.

There is a certain historical irony that a government run by shameless Oxbridge amateurs should so effectively condemn a local administration of which they had almost no first-hand knowledge. How were they able to preserve the myth so long? Partly because the long delay in local reform meant that local government was, as it is today, virtually unintelligible to the ordinary citizen. Sir George Goschen described the system as "a chaos as regards authorities, a chaos as regards rates, and a worse chaos as regards areas".[13] The theme of local inadequacy was again taken up by the Webbs. The most important volume of their monumental local government study is about the use of statutory authorities to circumvent local inefficiencies. Few reformers noticed that local government was never given a chance to perform. The Local Government Board of 1871 was a *pot pourri* of functions that no senior minister seemed to want, least of all poor law administration. Its most disastrous secretary was John Burns, once a firebrand in the labour movement, whose evangelical dedication persuaded him to ignore what few powers the Board had to improve local government.[14] The result was that the emerging new ministries for social reform could easily steamroller their way in Whitehall with minimal local consultation and with constant charges of local incompetence.

The mood changed in the 1960s but not in a way that would enable local government to withstand the Thatcher onslaught. On the contrary, the two Maude reports only confirmed long-standing central prejudices that the locals were inefficient and wasteful. A decade of labouring the importance of "effective" local government prepared the ground for Thatcher. While much of Europe was reorganizing local government in partnership with national government, Whitehall mandarins were preaching local inadequacies. The Royal Commissions on local government of the time happily echoed the Benthamite formula for rational government. A high-tech Heath followed a high-tech Wilson. A more adroit Prime Minister followed them but for his pains was destroyed by public sector unions, many of them controlling important local social services. A strange suicidal chorus follows as local government officials enthusiastically join the throng calling for more corporate planning, more efficient chief executives and more powerful local committees. No doubt Mrs Thatcher needs little prompting for her attack on local government but she was only pursuing with more vigilance than most

[13] Quoted in Redlich and Hirst, v. 1, 1903, p. 194.
[14] Kenneth D. Brown, *John Burns*, London, Royal Historical Society, 1977. Burns staunchly opposed Poor Law reform and essentially left the initiative in local government policy-making to the Board of Education and later to the Ministry of Health.

Prime Ministers the advice that had been consistently given for a much longer time. The extravagances of the militant local authorities only added credibility to arguments that had been developed in Westminster and Whitehall over the past twenty years.

In effect, British local government has been whiplashed between the complacent Labour platitudes that services should be equalized and Tory prejudices that strong local government is a menace. Most of this legislation has been Tory reaction to Labour neglect. The Local Government Act of 1929, for example, effectively closed the option of creating more boroughs to provide better local government for new urban concentrations. In 1972 Peter Walker effectively turned Labour's proposal on its head by imposing a two-tier system on metropolitan counties and unifying government in the shires. Much of suburban Britain was effectively neutralized by being absorbed into rural authorities. Urban authorities were left with an unwieldy division of powers between metropolitan counties and districts.[15] There followed a campaign by Peter Shore to restore unitary government to twenty or so former Labour strongholds among the abolished boroughs which was defeated largely because the local Labour organizations were exhausted from a decade of central government quarrelling over local government. By the mid-1970s the most controversial local area problems had been debated four times before parliamentary and Whitehall committees. Having produced so many unsatisfactory reforms over a decade, simply replacing local government with administrative boards and government regulations was no more than the next logical step.

Throughout this effort to rule local government from the centre it appeared unimaginable that the emperor might have no clothes. The Maude Commission, for example, was instructed not to study ministerial relations with local government, though the report did squeeze in about twenty tactful pages on the most controversial and least understood element in centre–local relations. With the largest local government areas in population terms of any democracy, local services still vary wildly from one part of Britain to another. The unexamined possibility, well known to French, Germans and Americans, was that areas and functions should sort themselves out by giving localities more discretion and arming local officials with a variety of organizational options. Much of the routine work of American local government is performed by district governments or semi-public corporations. The French have both single- and multi-purpose district agencies that are easily formed and easily dissolved. The Gaullist solution to local reorganization in the 1960s was simply to create an array of local service agencies and areas, including the new towns (now abolished), the metropolitan areas (seven

---

[15] Perhaps the most crippling was to give the urban districts primary planning authority in the metropolitan counties so that Britain emerged in 1972 with 500 planning authorities instead of 150 despite the territorial consolidation. The Housing Finance Act of the same year removed local power over rents.

communautés urbaines), a bewildering array of land-zoning agencies (each with different incentives), and of course the unified regional and urban powers given to Paris.[16] Apart from some vehemently condemned efforts to impose some of these schemes on communes and departments in the early 1960s, the local authorities were left to form their own combinations of areas and functions as they best saw their interests and as they themselves could agree about their futures.

This is not to suggest that the administrative powers of departmental and regional prefects were negligible, but these have almost always been exercised with more circumspection and care than even many Frenchmen realize. Even before the Socialist reforms of 1982, heavy-handed administration was discouraged. Upwardly mobile prefects did not want their careers botched by local political quarrels. Large cities and urban conglomerations necessarily began to handle much of their own business years ago. What differentiates the Socialist reform from British habits is that decentralization is conceived as a cumulative process. No doubt many mayors did not get all the responsibilities they hoped for but neither were their most important aims ignored. In the most centralized of national government functions, education, primary and secondary school management was devolved on departments. The planning process was simplified with lower levels given a clearer voice and mayors given the valuable political plum of issuing building permits. The entire system of local social services (*aide sociale*) was given to departments and communes, involving a transfer of about 30 billion francs from central to local budgets. The changes may not seem dramatic to a country where local authorities administer nearly all services. The difference is that these arrangements were not imposed from above but negotiated, accompanied with commensurate financial transfers, phased in with administrative support by knowledgeable civil servants and implemented without confrontation. What ultimately happens is up to the locals. One conservative department in the Loire, for example, has simply opted to leave everything in the hands of the prefect.[17] Small communes are free to assign their business to the prefects; large communes are already fighting to extend the powers they have been given.

Both French local officials and local councils see their relationship to the centre in terms of their capacity to grow and to adapt to new needs. The Crozier image of oppressed localities had some truth in the early 1960s but paradoxically it was de Gaulle's own insistence on modernizing

[16] While both the Labour and Conservative reorganization bills were monopolized by area debates the French have been relentless in creating new types of authorities, new contractual relationships and new lending arrangements to interlock national and local interests. See Ashford, *British Dogmatism and French Pragmatism*, pp. 329–337. Contrary to common belief, the small scale of the system is not a handicap but a virtue in facilitating negotiations for diverse programmes and objectives.

[17] Ashford, "Decentralizing France: How the Socialists Discovered Pluralism", NYU–Columbia University Conference, October 1987, to appear.

the French urban structure that effectively decentralized decision-making. In effect, the Socialists agreed with the Gaullists that there was no sense wasting more effort to consolidate small communes. French logic never presumed that common standards would work, or even that they would make much sense in a politically articulate intergovernmental system. But the liberated departmental councils as well as the old communal councils now have real discretionary powers. A major local victory contained in the *loi Defferre* was an ambiguous clause permitting localities to engage in economic activities. No one really knows what this means but neither are central officials snuffing out local economic experiments. Several more progressive towns in the Isère, for example, are joint partners in buy-outs and industrial ventures to create jobs. The centrist mayor of one large city, Nîmes, used his new powers to create a communal minimum income. In effect, France puts the intergovernmental network to work rather than define problems according to preferred outcomes. The French expect there to be variations among localities and national government does not pretend that it can solve every local solution. There have, of course, been partnerships for some British problems but they are most often of limited scope and size and carefully negotiated to meet Whitehall rules. Real partnerships exist when both parties help make the rules.

Few persons foresaw in 1980 that arbitrary controls on local spending and local taxation were only the tip of the Thatcher iceberg. The full dimensions of the Tory attack appeared in her third government when privatization shifted from public corporations and nationalized industries to service provision. Plans were launched to sell parts of the London Green Belt for commercial and industrial development. There has been legislation to divest local government of local colleges and polytechnics, no doubt because so many sociology graduates from these institutions became the core of radical left local councils. More subtle were schemes to persuade council house tenants to opt for private management agreements via Department of Environment "approved landlords". Special programmes for inner cities were coupled with proposals to divest these local councils of their responsibility for education in new "Crown schools". To add insult to injury, cuts in the block grant were calculated to meet the cost of inner city programmes and the dismantling of the GLC.[18] Local government was invited to its own funeral. A little noticed tribute to Thatcherite domination of the periphery was the simultaneous demise of President Reagan's "new federalism". His 1981 Omnibus Budget Reconciliation Act merged a number of intergovernmental transfers and looked forward to a further shift of federal programmes to state and local government.[19] After

[18] *Economist*, January 25, 1986.
[19] See General Accounting Office, *A Summary and Comparison of the Legislative Provisions of the Block Grants Created by the 1981 Omnibus Budget Reconciliation Act*, Washington DC, GAO, 1982.

stormy protests from mayors and governors "new federalism" was never mentioned again.

Local Resources: A One Man Band

The Layfield Committee popularized the phrase "he who pays the piper calls the tune". What the Layfield group failed to see was that there has always been but one piper in British government, the Treasury. When push comes to shove in hard times the Treasury will usually get its way. To be sure, the Treasury cannot hold the line when the economy is growing. During the 1950s and 1960s local spending grew at unbelievable rates in all the democracies. It was after all a Labour Party minister who said the "party is over" when the economic crisis of the 1970s hit home. In a much more loosely joined system of fiscal control, the American counties' and cities' spending became "uncontrollable",[20] oddly enough in no small measure because a conservative president, Nixon, hoped that giant new transfers to local government in the form of Food Stamps (to get the rural vote) and Revenue Sharing (to get the urban vote) would persuade Congress to pass the negative income tax. At about the same time, Giscard d'Estaing was implementing the first of several measures to bring French local taxation into line with Common Market agreements. His reform of the old local salary tax to produce the *taxe professionnel* (no less detested) is said to have cost the Ministry of Finance four billion francs in new local government allowances and transfers. In most countries the "piper" analogy makes no sense because the locals have a degree of fiscal autonomy commensurate with their responsibility and political clout. Layfield was right to opt for a more flexible resource but wrong in thinking the centre might accept a mutually beneficial solution to local resource problems. Fortunately, the Militant Tendency came at exactly the right moment to persuade Mrs Thatcher that local government was irretrievably profligate.

Intergovernmental negotiation of local spending and investment is impossible in a system of government that so clearly concentrates budgetary power in a single agency of government. The tradition of Treasury control is ancient. For much of the nineteenth century the fragmentation of local government concealed the problem, but even in 1835 Treasury officials saw to it that the municipal reform bill contained the provision that any borrowing by local authorities pass through their hands for approval. The tax issue was probably sealed in the late 1840s when it was decided that "personalty" did not include private wealth so that local taxation was effectively confined to real property.[21] But a century of landlord local government did not stop at such minor

---

[20] Martha Derthick, *Uncontrollable Spending*, Washington DC, The Brookings Institutions, 1974.

[21] Peel promised tax relief from the Contingency Fund in 1846 in order to reassure landowners they would not be hurt by Corn Law repeal. In 1817 land provided two-thirds

restrictions. The Local Government Act of 1894 removed half the value of agricultural land from local tax rolls. The Local Government Act of 1929 totally derated agricultural land. The persons whose political power had prevented the miserable Victorian cities from taxing landed wealth had their final revenge with Thatcher's spending and tax legislation. The standardization of non-domestic taxation in her third term will only complete the fiscal subordination of local government.

Part of the problem is, of course, the local authorities themselves who were lulled into complacency with massive increases in local grants for many years. Having so indiscriminately spent money to hide its weakness, one can hardly be surprised that the Treasury was just as eager to save money indiscriminately once it had political backing. For many years the local authorities were the beneficiaries of an adversarial tug of war over the nature of the grant. Aneurin Bevan himself once protested at the inequalities of local property evaluation, saying that local authorities should not "determine the size of the spoon with which they will scoop out Exchequer money".[22] The quixotic search for fiscal justice began when Labour hoped to equalize local incomes through standardized property evaluation in 1948 but no one gave much thought to new resources. Essentially both Tories and Labour agreed that local finance must be in lockstep with national finance. A surprisingly similar strategy inspired the Tories' "needs" formula in 1958 that hoped to judge independently what local authorities should receive. Two years later more stringent rules were issued for the determination of domestic and industrial (now euphemistically called "non-domestic") rates. Labour countered in 1966 by adding the "domestic element" to the grant formula, basically a rent subsidy, but still no new resources.

By then, of course, the grant system was unintelligible to any but the most carefully tutored, further isolating MPs, councillors and the public from understanding local government problems. But Thatcher's high-handed methods are hardly new. Since 1958 Whitehall has determined "relevant expenditure", the amount on which the total grant is based. Richard Crossman, the minister who launched local reorganization in 1966, had little to say when the Treasury axed local grants in 1968.[23] Britain was on a collision course long before the petrol crisis. In the 1960s the rate of increase of the grant was twice that of the GNP. Thus, it is quite misleading to identify Mrs Thatcher as a deviant in local finance. Both Tory and Labour ministers have been complaining about local spending for years and done nothing about it. As in the case of the now forgotten Royal Commission on Local Income Tax of 1901, the

of local tax revenues but by 1891 only fifteen per cent. H. Fowler, *Report of the Local Government Board*, London, House of Commons Papers, v. 58, 1893, p. xi.

[22] Quoted in K. B. Smellie, *A History of Local Government*, London, Allen and Unwin, 1968, p. 133.

[23] Richard Crossman, *Diaries of a Cabinet Minister*, London, Hamish Hamilton and Jonathan Cape, 1976, v. 2, p. 644.

final solution was always to dredge up more national revenue rather than permit localities to exercise their own fiscal judgment and take the consequences. More clearly than in any other illustration of arbitrary central power, the total nationalization of local finance has been in the making for fifty years. All Thatcher did was to come into the open.

French local taxation is probably no less complex than British. The difference is that mayors are mobilized by the multi-party system, the regional governments and eventually through the Senate ("la grande commune de France") to battle out local fiscal and tax problems. However much humbled by the *a priori* powers of prefects over local budgets, the French communes and departments have always known that their complaints would reach Paris. Indirect taxes were reformed by President Giscard d'Estaing and plans were made to consolidate many small local transfers into a single operating grant (*dotation globale de fonctionnement* or DGF). Until the oil crisis, the rates of increase of both direct and indirect local taxes were remarkably similar, not so much because the Ministry of Finance insisted on stable local finances, but because the local governments resisted tax increases in their own interests. Most local taxes do in fact become business taxes, so the wildly competitive communes had no desire to see local taxes soar. The more dense intergovernmental network provides a self-regulating check on local spending—something which seems unimaginable in Whitehall and which, of course, has now been made impossible by Thatcher. In any event, the crux of intergovernmental negotiation in France is not so much about current spending as about capital spending.

While British industry languished in the 1960s under the severe efforts to preserve the pound, de Gaulle made ambitious plans to modernize French cities and industry. Unlike Britain, where public investment was syphoned off to finance nationalized industries, centrally controlled new towns and the replacement of archaic hospitals, about two-thirds of French public investment filtered through the intergovernmental network. Despite the claims of inordinate central control, French economic growth over the 1960s was predicated on urban development. Naturally, there was an enormous struggle between the two branches of the field administration most likely to benefit,[24] but there was also substantial involvement of local government at all levels. Unlike Britain, France has a huge public investment bank, the Caisse des Dépôts, which developed large housing and infrastructure banking subsidiaries over the 1960s. Rather than squirrel away surpluses and unspent funds, French local budget surpluses and balances are mobilized for investment programmes with joint national, regional and local participation. The intricate system of intergovernmental bargaining has its shortcomings. In some communes the swimming pool can hold the entire population.

[24] On the struggle between the rural field service, the *génie rurale*, and the modern public works engineers, the *ponts et chaussées*, see J.-C. Thoenig, *L'Ere des technocrates: Le cas des ponts et chaussées*, Paris, Edition d'Organisation, 1973.

On the other hand, one big advantage of the Socialist government of the 1980s is that the cities and towns are not crying out for capital funds. While urban deterioration multiplies British inner city problems, the French mayors are relieved of capital expenditure needs for a decade or so. The French put growth to work for cities.

But the constant competition between communes and Paris meant that mayors were nonetheless demanding reform in the 1980s. Despite efforts to simplify loan procedures, there were enormous delays and capricious decisions. The Socialist addition to this system was to merge the local investment subsidy into a single grant (*dotation globale d'équipement* or DGE). In 1981 the DGE was about 3.5 billion francs, one-half of which was directly assigned to communal projects. The point is that a strong intergovernmental network means that local mayors, presidents of departmental councils, regional officials and newly elected deputies cannot be excluded from capital spending plans. It would be unimaginable in France, for example, to require new town residents to form a private housing management scheme if they preferred working with the local council. No French minister would dare to suggest that an established benefit, such as the 3.5 billion pound housing benefit that Thatcher considered partially unloading on local government, should be imposed without commensurate concessions to local government. Indeed, the French mayors extracted a price for the DGE, acquiring more control over land-zoning and the right to issue building permits.

The more stratified and differentiated French local government system is in many respects better able to adjust to local government becoming big business than the over-centralized and arbitrary British system. One of the most hotly contested sections of the *loi Defferre* was to abolish *a priori* administrative approval of local budgets. Prefects have the right to guard their flanks. They are free to lodge a complaint where they think there are major violations of financial rules, but from 1983 they no longer ruled on local budgets until the end of the fiscal year. Naturally this produced apprehensions in Paris so that there is now a new *grands corps*, a regional *cour des comptes* or audit service that will examine the local budgets. (There was a comic moment when the Parisian Cour des Comptes refused to relocate in the provinces which required the formation of a new *grands corps* for the countryside.) In effect, the mayors settled for what any vigorous, self-respecting local official wants: a fair hearing. Whether *a priori* or *a posteriori* auditing makes any difference in an era of multi-million dollar local budgets is another question, but Paris went a long way toward removing one of the most intense local grievances.

The Tortoise and the Hare

My study tracing the odd consistency with which both Westminster and Whitehall ignore the intricacies of local politics and local administration produced some sceptical reviews in Britain. Left-leaning reformers wanted more unreserved condemnation of Tory manipulation; right-leaning conservatives wanted more acknowledgement of how local government can damage national interests. The common feature of both positions was to blame failures, inefficiency or neglect on local government alone. My forecast came true when irresponsible militants took over several large cities in order to conduct guerilla war against London while Mrs Thatcher used Westminster and Whitehall to smother British local government. Adversarial politics disgraced both local government and local democracy.

The price of high-handed policy-making, so easily accomplished in a stable, strong parliament, is that the nation deprives itself of one of its most important assets. Local government is not simply about equal provision of services or holding down national debt. The purpose of an intergovernmental network is to balance national and local interests. If there is no limit to national demands then local discretion and eventually local self-respect wither. Worse perhaps, local government cannot conduct experiments to solve new problems, to diffuse social crises or to mobilize public support. Time will tell whether Thatcher has accomplished in eight years what fifty years of reform failed to do. Local government is now thoroughly politicized and large numbers of MPs, including many loyal Tories, are outraged. Perhaps their alarm will provide the occasion to develop the mutual respect which effective intergovernmental politics presupposes.

Britain and France are polar opposites in interesting ways. The Revolution enshrined the commune at a time when the British landed aristocracy were ruthlessly protecting their local patronage in the counties. Having staked its political future on the rationality of citizens, French government needed a century to make mass democracy work. The commune was an integral part of the democratization of France. (A disastrous 1971 plan to consolidate communes permitted the mayors to continue as honorary officials complete with red, white and blue sashes.) Having staked its future on aristocratic abilities to contain absolute monarchy, the British historical problem was how to subordinate counties and boroughs to landed interests. For France, a vigorous intergovernmental network was essential; for Britain, a strong inter-governmental network was initially superfluous and later a menace to parliamentary supremacy. An intergovernmental network without discretion is either a fraud or a tyranny. For many years national policy-makers, often with local compliance, decided to make a sham of local government. In this respect, Thatcher accurately assessed the situation.

The important question is whether Britain's local government can be restored without reverting to its old bad habits. First, the Audit Commission has shown that the next government is likely to inherit a local government structure even more dramatically divided into rich and poor areas than emerged from a century of ruthless capitalism and industrial growth.[25] Instead of having priorities for inner cities, enterprise zones and unemployed youth centrally defined and regulated, perhaps local governments might be asked to design their own programmes. Second, it is clear that local government is building up a huge concealed deficit in terms of deferred purchase agreements, estimated at 4.5 billion pounds in 1987, and foolish operational charges to capital budgets of about a billion pounds. Perhaps it is time to treat local authorities like sensible bodies and allow them to rescue themselves with a selection of new revenue sources. Third, perhaps Labour leaders should stop talking about all the tasks that local government will *have to do* when they return to power[26] and simply ask their long neglected local organizations to begin to make their own plans. Labour Party neglect of local politics helped put Mrs Thatcher in power. It would be a sad commentary to see one tyranny replace another.

[25] *Times*, January 29, 1987, reporting on the Audit Commission, *The Management of London's Authorities: Preventing the Breakdown of Services*, London, HMSO, 1987, and August 4, 1986, on Ridley's protest over the Japanese loan to Liverpool.
[26] Speech by Roy Hattersley, *Times*, April 24, 1986.

DOES INDUSTRIAL POLICY MATTER? LAND GOVERNMENTS IN RESEARCH AND TECHNOLOGY POLICY IN FEDERAL GERMANY

JOSEF ESSER*

Since the start of the 1980s it has been possible to discern various activities in the field of industrial policy at the level of the Länder of Federal Germany, and these differ both quantitatively and qualitatively from those of the 1960s and 1970s. This raises the question whether, at this period of economic and social upheaval, there is at the *territorial* level a shift from the central state to that of regional authorities in the formulation and implementation of industrial policy. Can one speak of an "awakening of the regions"?[1] Quite apart from this question, from the point of view of the theory of the state it is also important to establish what role is being played by the Länder in the introduction and social articulation of new technologies in the predominantly privately owned economy of the Federal Republic.

To put the matter differently: does political decision-making have any real impact on the goal definition, evaluation and development of the so-called "key technologies", or does political activity here at Land level amount to nothing more than symbolic politics? If the latter, what is the function of this symbolic politics? Since the Land governments are of various party-political characters, it is also of interest whether this factor makes any difference. Finally, there is an interesting question concerning party differences and corporatist politics: do Länder governments of different parties develop different patterns of co-operation between state, capital and trade unions, and do these have distinct implications for economic modernisation?

These questions have been the focus of a research project which is examining decision mechanisms and priorities in industrial policy in

* Professor Esser teaches political science at the University of Frankfurt am Main. He is the author of several studies of the politics of industrial policy in the Federal Republic. This essay has been translated for *The Political Quarterly* by Colin Crouch.

[1] Report of the Bulling Commission on a new leadership structure for Baden-Württemberg (*Neue Führungsstruktur Baden-Württemberg*), Stuttgart, 1985.

94

three Länder: Baden-Württemberg, Hessen and Nordrhein-Westfalen.[2] The project is not yet completed, so the following amounts to an interim report.

Plan of the Research

In choosing industrial policy as the object of study we have to consider fashionable theories that, as a result of technical changes at both macro- and micro-levels, industrial society is undergoing transition to a "post-industrial" or "service-economy" or "information" society. We have taken the view that the idea of a *third phase of the industrial revolution*[3] better describes the situation: the industrial capitalist nature of western society is being modified but not transcended. This third phase involves the installation of new "key technologies" in all sectors and branches of the economy. The distinctive characteristics of these technologies are that they: (i) lead to a large number of new products and production methods; (ii) apply to a large number of economic sectors; (iii) provide the technical basis for overcoming the apparent stagnation, contradictions and social conflicts that had been created by the growth pattern of post-war capitalism. (That is, they help to economise on both labour and capital, to enable both to be used more flexibly, to economise in the use of raw materials and energy, and to cause less damage to the environment than previous technologies.)[4]

In this way micro-electronics, bio-technology and new materials are all examples of the new "key technologies". Micro-electronics finds applications in semi-conductors, telecommunications, industrial robots, computers, new machine tool construction (computer-aided design, computer-aided manufacturing, computer-integrated manufacturing), and in software. Biotechnology has applications in genetic engineering, biological cell technology, bioprocess engineering. New materials are used in changes in both products and production methods. These three technologies are marked out as strategically important by their interdependence. Often progress in one stimulates progress in the other two.

There is no space here to consider whether such a process of change *within* industrial society is central to restructuring in all advanced western economies.[5] But in Germany there is widespread consensus that in the current period of disturbance, which has created intensified

---

[2] In addition to the author the other participants in the project were Bertold Huber and Jutta Wache-Symalla.

[3] L. and I. Hack, *Die Wirklichkeit, die Wissenschafft*, Frankfurt am Main, 1985.

[4] B. van Tulder and G. Junne, *European Multinationals in Core Technologies*, 1988.

[5] It would, for example, be interesting to investigate whether such countries as the UK and the USA have declined in international competition because they have concentrated excessively on extending the service sector and have therefore allowed the manufacturing base to erode (see J. Esser and G. Ziebura, *Europa am Scheideweg*, Frankfurt am Main, forthcoming).

competition among nation-states, the pattern of specialisation combined with sectoral coherence should be defended and extended further.[6] The pattern has, after all, been so successful in the past. In detail, this approach has a number of implications.

First, on the basis of the micro-electronic and information technology revolutions, those sectors that were so central to success in the 1960s and 1970s—machine tools, construction equipment, vehicles, chemicals, oil processing, artificial fibres, electronics, optical electronics—should become further modernised, specialised and flexibilised. Second, since from the outset the Federal German economy was characterised by a close mutual integration of all branches of industry, extending both to small and medium-sized enterprises and to the service sector (banks, insurance, marketing, export assistance), this process should be extended even further. Third, to the extent that they provide important functions for the central export sectors, traditional sectors such as steel, textiles, clothing and clock-making should also become modernised, specialised and flexibilised.

The guiding vision of the Federal Republic is extended further: the modernisation of the industrial sector is the basis of a sound economy; therefore industrial policy is not just one field of politics among others, but has strategic significance for the development of the whole society. We can distinguish three dimensions of industrial policy: (i) state infrastructure provision in the widest sense, that is, all measures directed at adaptation, renewal and restructuring of the productive apparatus; (ii) state integration and legitimation activity, that is, measures aimed at securing social consensus in setting the goals for structural change and in establishing strategies for the state's role in interest intermediation and conflict regulation; (iii) forms of social and political organisation that are necessary in order to bind together the policies established under (i) and (ii).

The three Länder studied in the project were chosen because they were at the time of their selection governed by different parties: in Baden-Württemberg the Christian Democratic Union (CDU), in Nordrhein-Westfalen the Social Democrats (SPD), and in Hessen between 1985 and 1987 a coalition of the SPD and the Greens. All three Länder are, however, similar in size, economic and social structure, so that distortions in comparability from such sources were excluded as much as possible. Because the SPD-Green coalition in Hessen broke down after two years our material for this Land is too thin to include it systematically in the comparison, so the following account concentrates on the other two Länder and refers to Hessen only sporadically.

Two types of analysis have been undertaken: an extensive one tracing the policy content, prevailing state integration and legitimation policy and the social and political organisation of industrial policy; and an

[6] J. Esser, "State, Business and Trade Unions in West Germany after the 'Political Wende'", *West European Politics*, vol 9, no 2, April 1986, pp. 198–214.

intensive one concentrating on an individual branch of industry to determine whether different political conceptions will have different effects by originating and developing new technologies in this branch at Land level. In this interim report it is possible to consider only the former.

Co-operative Federalism and Policy Integration

It is difficult to establish a clear division of labour between the federal and Land level.[7] True, the Constitution (or Basic Law) envisages a distinction in legislative competence between exclusive and shared areas. It gives the Federal Government alone responsibility for foreign policy, defence, citizen rights, currency, Federal boundaries, railways, air transport, posts and telecommunications, and central police functions. In the case of areas of shared jurisdiction the Länder have the right to legislate unless and until the Federal Government makes use of its own right to do so. It can do this in three different circumstances: when the legislation of individual Länder is not effective; where the law of a Land affects the interests of other Länder or the country as a whole; or, in the terms of the Basic Law, "where protection of the legal or economic unity, in particular protection of the unity of conditions of life over the territory of a Land so demands".

This third provision has been seen as the Trojan horse of centralism within the federal system, and has been the basis on which the Federal Government has taken to itself responsibility for virtually all policy areas—above all foreign policy, and also legal, economic, agricultural, transport and social policy. Left to the Länder alone are just education policy and administrative structure.[8]

These centralising tendencies reached their apogee following the important recession of 1966–67, when a strengthened offensive on the world market by the German economy in order to overcome the crisis was interpreted as an overwhelming necessity. The entry of the SPD into the Government made possible the construction of forms and institutions of state intervention deemed necessary to achieve this goal. After the extension of Keynesian mechanisms introduced in the Stability Law and the strengthened inclusion of the trade unions in state opinion-formation and decision-making processes, the most important innovation was a further centralisation and rationalisation of federalism. The aim here was to overcome the "distorting" impact of regional and local institutions. In particular the financial autonomy of Länder and local authorities was reduced, the legislative and administrative authority of the central state was extended, and an attempt was made to secure co-ordination of overall policy through a

[7] T. Ellwein and J. J. Hesse, *Das Regierungssystem der Bundesrepublik Deutschland*, 6, revised and extended edition, Opladen, 1987, pp. 77 ff.
[8] *Ibid.* p. 78.

reform that supervened the planning and administrative powers of these lower tier authorities with such new central institutions as the Finance Planning Council, the Economic Management Council and regional planning associations. The most important results of this "vertical policy integration" were the newly established communal projects for the improvement of agricultural structure, coastal protection, the improvement of regional economic structure, the extension of further education and the improvement of policy for education and research.

But the centralisation was just one side of the coin. The involvement of the Länder in legislation and in administrative federalism permanently forces the Federal Government to co-operate with them in many ways. As a result one cannot describe German federalism in terms of an unambiguous hierarchy of superior and inferior levels, but must speak of "co-operative federalism"[9] and "policy integration".[10] By administrative federalism one means that the Federal Government is provided with its own administrative apparatus in only a few exceptional areas, while in the remainder Federal laws are implemented by the Länder. The latter are therefore immediately involved in federal legislation, in particular through the Bundesrat, the second chamber of parliament, which is part of the legislation process. At least half of Federal legislation has to have the consent of the Bundesrat. The Bundesrat comprises representatives of the executives of the Länder, not their parliaments as such.

Under these circumstances co-operative federalism and policy integration are necessary conditions for the functioning of federal politics. From the outset, ongoing, bureaucratically competent administrative authorities of the Länder participate in the policy-making process, which not always but often enough has an impact on the legislative process. In this process the Federal Government has to sound out what will be acceptable to the Länder. A bureaucratic consensus is constructed, which sometimes enables the Federal level to take over a Land competence, provided the rights of the Bundesrat and the administrative autonomy of the Länder are respected. This form of policy integration increased in importance after 1969, as more and more communal tasks were defined that legally could be managed only through consensus between the two levels.

In the fields of economic structure and education and research, this technocratic planning model for joint tasks sought to combine in the most efficient possible way the power and finance resources of the central state with the information base and administrative capacity of the Länder.[11] But no sooner was it established when the crisis for which it would be most needed broke: the world economic crisis of the mid-

[9] G. Lehmbruch, *Parteienwettbewerb im Bundesstaat*, Stuttgart, 1976.

[10] F. Scharpf, B. Reissert and F. Schnabel, *Politikverflechtung*, Kronberg, 1976.

[11] D. Garlichs, "Grenzen zentralstaatlicher Planung in der Bundesrepublik", in H. Wollmann (ed), *Politik im Dickicht der Bürokratie*, Opladen, 1979, pp. 71–102.

1970s. While the central state was reducing the scope for regional financial assistance, the conflict between Länder over regional priority aid grew. The level of consensus between Bund and Länder declined, with a blocked decision-making process as a result.[12] True, the Länder did not desert the pursuit of joint tasks with the Federal Government. To the contrary, the blockage occurred because in each Land so many areas were put forward for special help that it was not possible to allocate priorities sensibly.[13] The Länder were forced into harsher competition over industrial location, offering financial deals, administrative help, their own assistance programmes, tax breaks, subsidies and technology parks. Vertical policy integration was being supplemented by an attempt by each Land to acquire its own special industrial policy profile. Each wanted to be the acme of technical innovation and progress.

Research Findings

Our research included discussions with Land ministries, chambers of industry and trade, business associations, unions, parties and so-called para-state institutions. So far we can offer the following conclusions.

Multinational firms as the central actors

The main agents in the introduction and development of new techniques lie within the private economy itself, in particular the giant multi-nationals. State industrial policy makes no *substantive* contribution to the discovery and development of techniques. Rather, the important calculations here are made by those firms that have to maintain their own international competitiveness and profitability. This can be seen from the crude figures: in 1987 61 % of all resources for research and development in the Federal Republic came from the private sector, and 71 % of R & D was carried out by firms themselves. Further, the state share has been diminishing over the years. In 1981 the financial contribution of Bund and Länder together was 42.5 %; by 1987 it was only 37.7 %.[14] Those sectors that are important for the employment of research staffs and general economic wealth creation of the Federal Republic have largely provided their own resources for R & D. The share ranges from 98 % in chemicals to 89 % in electronics.[15]

The Government's research report for 1988[16] shows that research in

[12] Scharpf, *op cit.*
[13] W. Väth, *Raumplanung*, Königstein, 1980; W. Bruder and T. Ellwein (eds), *Raumordnung und staatliche Steuerungsfähigkeit*, PVS-Sonderheft 10/1979, Opladen, 1980; P. Klemmer, *Regionalpolitik auf dem Prüfstand*, Cologne, 1986.
[14] Bundesminister für Forschung und Technologie, *Bundesbericht Forschung 1988*, Bonn, 1988, p. 60.
[15] *Ibid*, p. 86.
[16] *Ibid*, p. 99.

the private sector is concentrated almost entirely in the large firms, while middle-sized enterprises concern themselves mainly with development and construction. In 1978 only 500 or so small and medium-sized firms undertook their own R & D; the number has now risen to 20,000. By 1985 such firms were contributing 17 % of total R & D effort. In particular, small firms which had close relations with large companies were often deeply involved in the R & D activities of those companies. In this connection it is interesting to note that R & D activity in the "key technologies" and their application is often carried out by large concerns in co-operation, whether at national, European or global level.[17] How this "private" industrial policy of the giant firms works, what institutions exist for co-operation and conflict regulation, has so far not been the subject of social science research.

The content of state infrastructure activity

There is no discernible difference in the content of infrastructure activity in the various Länder. It is everywhere governed by the imperatives of the private sector. In detail the following measures are identifiable:

(i) special programmes to encourage developments in the so-called future-oriented technology fields: micro-electronics, information and communication technology, biotechnology, production and manufacturing technologies, transport and raw materials technologies;

(ii) extension of regional research capacities in higher education institutions outside the universities to extend scientific research and to direct the emphasis of research programmes towards future-oriented technologies;

(iii) linkage of so-called basic research with applied research and development including establishment of links between university research and the private economy;

(iv) increased competition over the establishment and location of major research institutes;

(v) improving the efficiency of regional technical innovation systems including extension of innovation advisory services for the economy, intensification of technology transfers, especially for small and medium-sized firms;

(vi) new means for encouraging the foundation of technology-oriented firms through special centres and technology parks;

(vii) special programmes for the integration of industrial and service sectors, mainly through telecommunications policy;

(viii) the introduction of state procurement policies for the encouragement of new technical products.

In general it is possible to say that all three Länder are particularly

[17] van Tulder and Junne, op cit.

concerned to help small and medium-sized firms become equipped with the infrastructural prerequisites for continuing successfully to play their part in a partnership with larger concerns. These firms have in any case been traditionally closely bound up with such concerns. That also means, however, that those small firms that do not become involved in innovation will be left out of state help and will go under.

As instruments of this kind of small-industry policy, para-state institutions are established or reorganised: the Steinbeis Foundation in Baden-Württemberg, ZENIT (Centre for Innovation and Technology Ltd) in Nordrhein-Westfalen, the Hessen Land Development Trust Company (HLT). These in turn work closely with the technology advice and technology transfer centres of the Chambers of Industry and Trade as well as with private technology consultants.

A particularly effective but typical example is the Steinbeis Foundation. With the aid of a budget of some 30 million DM the Institute has helped teachers in science and engineering at the Land Fachhochschulen and universities to become "scientific entrepreneurs". They offer their innovative knowledge of the discovery and introduction of new products or production methods to private firms in the region. As these are adopted they establish a network of technology advice and transfer at the regional level. If they fail, the Steinbeis Foundation takes back its assistance. In this way numerous regional technology networks are established in the whole Land between private business and higher education. Although the Steinbeis Foundation was established under private law, it is linked closely to state research and technology policy through its director, who is at the same time technology commissioner in the Land government and has a place in the Land Economics Ministry and cabinet.

A comparison of state integration and legitimation efforts

Despite various criticisms of detail, businessmen in all three Länder have accepted this form of technology policy. Of course, they do so only because the Land governments enable business leaders, and especially members of the large firms, to be represented in joint councils, discussion circles, expert commissions that formulate the details of state policy. If ever a government strikes out with an initiative of its own, the business camp threatens boycotts, which then lead to withdrawal of the proposed measures. The Land level industry associations act here as permanently active "ideological warning stations". But how are conflicts among sections of private business handled? Here our research suggests that the highly organised structure of private business, through branch associations and the publicly established Chambers of Industry and Trade, work highly successfully.

In Nordrhein-Westfalen and for a time in Hessen there have been attempts to incorporate trade unions, works councils and employees into this innovation-oriented industrial policy, through the idea of "socially responsive technology". In Nordrhein-Westfalen this has been based on the traditionally strong trade unions, on which the Land government depended. The programme was established to run from 1984–88 within the industrial policy initiative "future technologies". About 100 research groups, financed with some 60 million DM, were given the task of "orienting new information and communications technologies and key areas of micro-technology according to people's needs in human, social and natural contexts, in their applications in production, exchange and the external environment".[18] The research fields chosen were "work and economy", "industrial work", "service sector and administration", "everyday life", "citizen and state", "dimensions of social responsibility". A joint committee representing the Government, science and important social groups proposes projects for selection and support by the Minister of Labour. A research institute on "Work and Technology" is also planned.

In fact what this initiative provides is a basis for a public dialogue over scientific research that brings together the important social groups and those affected by new technology, so that they can consider how the advantages and disadvantages of different new techniques affect various interests. True, the programme is unable either to be integrated with existing Land support programmes for introducing new technologies or to interfere with employers' autonomy in the introduction of new techniques; it is rather regarded by private industry as an unimportant "titbit for the unions".

A similar institution for establishing a public dialogue was planned in Hessen, through a "Hessen Forum on Information Technology and Society", consisting of a council of experts and a centre. The council of experts was to present a report every two years to the Land parliament and government, which would present a survey of the condition and development of information technology. It was envisaged as an advisory body for government and parliament. It would be the task of the centre to establish a dialogue with those affected by new technology. Both institutions were to draw public attention to the problems of new technology. Here too there was no question of interfering with the autonomy of private business.

In Baden-Württemberg there has up to now been no systematic policy for incorporating the unions. However, the Land government is careful to have informal specific contact with individual unions, even when it ignores the DGB's Land-level organisation. Consensus with the unions is usually sought through the numerous joint councils and expert commissions in which various union representatives—albeit chosen by

---

[18] Minister für Arbeit, Gesundheit und Soziales des Landes NRW, "Landesinitiative Zukunftstechnologien—Sozialverträgliche Technikgestaltung. Materialien zum Programm", mimeo., Düsseldorf, 1985.

the Land government—sit. Their representation and influence are much smaller than those of the employers.

Research into the consequences of technology was not an issue until 1987, when it achieved a particular meaning with the establishment of the Ulm Research Centre. This new and spectacular attempt to combine both organisationally and in content the activities of state, university, Fachhochschulen and extra-university research centres with the private interests of a few firms of various sizes, also included an expert commission on the evaluation of the consequences of technology. This had previously occupied itself with the definition of possible research themes in the fields of biotechnology, medical technology, information and communications technology as well as production and transport technologies. From this has emerged discussion over the establishment of an academy

> that could work with interested parties from both state and private sectors on research into the consequences of technology. In dialogue with the other expert commissions it would be established how the special aspects of the evaluation of consequences could be brought into present and future teaching arrangements.[19]

This change of thinking by the Baden-Württemberg Land government can partly be explained in terms of the need to win the support of the influential Land organisation of IG Metall for the "science city" project at Ulm—a project that was expensive and put other regions and universities in the Land at a disadvantage and was therefore politically controversial. Second, it also wanted to take up the proposal that had emerged from big industry that research into the consequences of technology should no longer be hindered, but should be taken up by scientists, engineers and technologists working *within* the private sector and therefore kept under control and not left to uncontrollable social scientists.

Social and political organisation compared

There are large differences in the social and political organisation of industrial policy in the three Länder studied, though it needs to be said at the outset that in no Land does the government achieve a controlling or even a political shaping function. In practice all three governments behave like the management of a business: the general policy of each is oriented to the conditions and requirements of the Land as an industrial location engaged in technological competition within and without the Federal Republic. In particular it was the task of state industrial policy to ensure politically the contents and development of a technology

---

[19] Policy statement on Forschungszentrum Ulm by Minister President Lothar Späth to the Landtag of Baden-Württemberg, Stuttgart, mimeo., Stuttgart, 17 September, 1987.

policy as defined by private firms. None of the three Land governments has yet acquired the competence to make its own evaluations.

Within these general similarities, the governments of Baden-Württemberg and of Nordrhein-Westfalen differ in the extent to which they have constructed a centralised state organisation for policy formation and decision. The short-lived experiment of the SPD-Green coalition in Hessen did not have enough time to implement the plans they had formulated for the development of ministerial organisation. Most significant was the attempt in Baden-Württemberg to concentrate all important discussions and decisions in the State Ministry, that is, in the office of the Minister President, and to overcome fragmentation into many departments. To develop this aim, in summer 1984 an expert commission was established on a "new leadership structure for Baden-Württemberg" under the chairmanship of Herr Bulling, president of the city council in Stuttgart. The commission also contained a representative of local government and two high-ranking businessmen. Minister President Späth established the need for the Commission in the following way:

> The currently growing need for policy to be better informed and to bring together the various social interests to a viable consensus makes necessary the establishment of new structures of leadership and communications. The administration must therefore acquire, with the help of an information technology system, the competence to deal with and integrate differentiated areas of knowledge and from that process to secure information that can be used to give leadership.[20]

A large number of needs had to be integrated: the needs for information, for communication, for co-operation, for flexibility, for decisions, for long-term planning.[21]

The commission reported in 1985. Its recommendations can be interpreted as a model of a new form of state, oriented to increasing the efficiency of industrial policy in a privately owned capitalist society in order to meet the combined technical, economic and social challenges of the third phase of the industrial revolution. The recommendations included proposals in the following areas.

Seven ministries of broadly equal importance for specific, clearly defined areas of policy should be established; in this way the traditional client relations between ministries and particular interests would be broken up and reorganised in ways appropriate to the new circumstances. A new Environment Ministry would take care of all ecological problems and interests; an Economics Ministry would deal with all interests concerned with research and technology, with economic development and foreign trade. A new Ministry for Communications and Arts would integrate in new ways new media, new

[20] Späth, L., *Wende in die Zukunft*, Reinbek bei Hamburg, 1985, p. 235.
[21] *Ibid*, p. 233.

communications technologies and "old" communications forms as well as the arts. A new Ministry for Social Policy would be the focus for all plans and issues affecting social policy. Each ministry should contain a new basic division, and each of these should work closely with the "supreme basic division" of the State Ministry, in order to prevent negative co-ordination and to increase the steering capacity of the centre. In order to improve information and control "from above", the whole Land administration should be linked together through a "Land system concept".[22] The leading personnel should receive an elite training in a new administrative college and should qualitatively improve their competence through frequent rotation. New specialised state agencies should guide technology installation and export activities across the Land. So-called "vision circles" should be established on the Japanese model. These should comprise independent persons from the fields of politics, administration, science and economy; they should be allocated to each ministry and should work to establish a general picture of feasible and desirable future developments.

Until now, strong conflicts with the state apparatus and affected interests have hindered the overall implementation of this new central structure. Nevertheless, the Minister President has succeeded in implementing the "Land system concept" and founding the new administrative college. In addition the ten existing ministries have been constrained in their competences and each must relinquish a specified number of functions and divisions. In that way the reconstruction of the ministries can be achieved from within. The resources of personnel thereby released become a pool which the Minister President can use as a flexible reserve in order to staff important areas of work. At the same time identically structured basic divisions were established in each ministry, which in particular have taken over the tasks of long-term planning, co-ordination and publicity. They work closely with a newly established department in the State Ministry on "planning and basic questions". Also, each ministry has been equipped with a scientific advisory circle, which in particular shall bring "expertise" from the economy and from science into the administration. All who can provide services for the Land's firms, including the Land's institute for technology transfer and the Steinbeis Foundation, have been concentrated in a spacious "Economy House".

Meanwhile it must be said that so far the Minister President has not succeeded politically in carrying through the overall centralisation and integration of the Land administration. However, the reforms carried out so far make possible the gradual fulfilment of the centralisation process. A clear loss of power from the Ministries of Science and Economy in favour of the State Ministry is already clear.

---

[22] H. F. Lorenz, "Neue Führungsstruktur und Landsystemkonzept. Innovationsmanagement in Baden-Württemberg", in *Der Bürger im Staat*, 1/1986, pp. 50–53, 1986.

A new "Land initiative for future technologies" was also planned in Nordrhein-Westfalen, as an all-embracing industrial policy concept incorporating all ministries, to enable the Land government to develop a planned approach to its "future-oriented infrastructure policy", "a policy for the planned shaping of structural change". Economic, technology and research policy were to be combined closely with environmental protection policy and social responsibility. Alongside the corporatist incorporation of trade unions and employers associations in various joint committees, the state administration would construct an interministerial planning group, the leadership of which would be in the State Chancellry, the office of the Minister President. As in Baden-Württemberg the aim was to co-ordinate the new industrial policy over the heads of traditional client interests in individual ministries through a central co-ordination in the State Chancellry. However, this centralising aim collapsed completely. Verbally the idea of integration and co-ordination was maintained, but in fact individual agencies developed their programmes in co-operation with their former clients. The Economics Ministry looks after the advancement of future technologies and technology transfer; the Science Ministry attends to technologically oriented front-line research in the universities and Fachhochschulen; the Labour Ministry is responsible for the programme "socially responsible technical development"—a programme in which the unions are primarily interested; the Environment Ministry supports ecologically responsible programmes; the City Construction Ministry the renovation and development of towns. This victory of individual agency egoisms over the attempts at co-ordination can be explained in terms of the stronger fragmentation and organising skills of social interests who learned long ago how to establish themselves successfully in various ministries.

Conclusion

This is as far as our empirical research can at present take us. It enables us to give certain answers to the questions raised at the outset. It is clear that during the 1980s the industrial policy activities of the German Länder have intensified, and that at that level a large number of innovative programmes have been developed for the advancement of technological development, technology transfer as well as socially responsible technological planning. There have also been attempts to make institutional and procedural changes in state machinery in order to meet the conditions for effective information adoption and working; the combination of resources, co-ordination and centralisation of competences and decisions; and the improvement of consensus building and conflict regulation. True, the latter failed in Nordrhein-Westfalen, while in Baden-Württemberg the outlines of some kind of technocratically

106

centralised state can be discerned, over the democratic credentials of which opinion is divided.

In spite of this the thesis of a transfer of functions from the level of the central state to that of the Länder cannot be sustained. The Federal Government has also, since the mid-1970s, extended its industrial policy activities, especially in the field of R & D. And here even bald figures show that there can be no talk of a decline in the functions of the federal level: its share of R & D expenditure was 26.3 % in 1981 and 24.3 % in 1987, while during the same period the share of the Länder dropped from 16.2 % to 13.4 %. About 71 % of Länder R & D spending went to the universities, and only 5 % to private firms; the Länder kept 24 % for their own research activities and for joint projects with the Federal Government in extra-university research establishments.[23]

However, more important are two further facts. First, in spite of the increase in their own activities the Länder have not renounced the model of co-operative federalism, but have engaged themselves in a variety of ways even further into the mechanisms of policy interlocks. Second, as we have seen, large companies play the strategically central role in introducing and shaping the contents of the new key technologies in the production process. And their activities are not bounded by Land, federal or even European levels, but operate world-wide. Their aim is the successful "insider" position in the triangle of the growth market comprising Japan, Europe and the USA.[24] And their research and development activities are similarly globally directed.[25] For these firms, therefore, the industrial political activities of German Länder are only to be interpreted as components of globally directed calculations of profit. Länder programmes, federal German programmes, European programmes (e.g. Esprit, Eureka, Brite, Race, ESA) are only as important as transnational co-operation with other European or Japanese or US competitors.[26] These global perspectives of the giant firms also explain why there can be no difference in the content of Länder programmes.

The only active role of the Länder—and here we come to the second question concerning their function in introducing and shaping new technologies in the private sector's production process—lies elsewhere. First, they can create the infrastructure and organisational prerequisites whereby small and medium-sized firms in the Länder can either operate as partners for the multinationals or can occupy niches in the world market by staying competent and efficient in production technology and work organisation. Most important for this is technology transfer between research in universities and other institutions and the medium-

[23] Bundesminister für Forschung und Technologie, *op cit*, pp. 66 ff.
[24] K. Ohmae, *Macht der Triade*, Wiesbaden, 1985.
[25] van Tulder and Junne, *op cit*.
[26] *Ibid*.

sized firm sector. The means used here are the classic ones: money and law.

Second, Land policy plays an active role in regulating conflict and ensuring legitimacy. Here we can distinguish between the right-wing corporatism of Baden-Württemberg and the left-wing corporatism of Nordrhein-Westfalen (to which latter the red-green model in Hessen would also have approximated). Right corporatism makes as much use of numerous joint committees and expert commissions as the leftist version. In both we find representatives of the economy, science and the unions with private firms in unchallenged leadership. One difference consists in the fact that the presence of the unions is far more restricted in Baden-Württemberg than in Nordrhein-Westfalen, informal and situation-specific consultation with unions being more important than their formal inclusion in explicit bodies.

The second difference is that in Nordrhein-Westfalen themes like "socially responsible technology planning" and "ecological and economic modernisation of the Land" are formally politicised[27] and provided with explicit programmes, in which the unions as organisations are given an important and politically officially recognised function, extending to determining the content and selection of projects. In contrast, in Baden-Württemberg conflict regulation is preferably shorn of politics and ideology in the social project of the harmonious "activity and reconciliation society",[28] a variant of "technocratic conservatism". This expects the new key technologies to extend as far as the reconciliation of ecology and economy and the solution of all social problems (unemployment, deskilling, new poverty, social division). The social democratic project of the "solidarity of reason" accepts a large number of conflicts, but believes that through the co-operative working together of all social groups a Kantian reason can become obvious to all.

As the established means of implementation in both right and left technocorporatism one finds "procedural steering".[29] The social function of this symbolic politics which plays a role in all three Länder can be characterised as an attempt to ensure the acceptance of new technology by those affected by it.

Does industrial policy matter? Our comparison suggests that, in a restricted sense, it does: not in the content of state infrastructure activities, but through political organisation and state legitimation and integration efforts. Unanswered remains the question of the contribution that is made by trade union participation. This will only be resolved when an intensive analysis has been carried out of industrial policy effects in a selected branch of industry.

[27] V. Ronge, *Forschungspolitik als Strukturpolitik*, Munich, 1977.
[28] Späth, 1985, *op cit.*
[29] C. Offe, *Berufsbildungsreform*, Frankfurt am Main, 1975.

REGIONAL ECONOMIC POLICY
IN ITALY

LINDA WEISS*

APART from providing one more instance of a trend running counter to centralist Britain, what makes the Italian experience of regionalism especially interesting? For some, it is the sheer novelty of sub-national authorities in a unitary state undertaking policy activities normally monopolised by the centre. For, as the title of this paper suggests, decentralisation in Italy has entailed much more than the management of social and territorial policy. Increasingly, since their establishment in the 1970s, regional governments have emerged as the planners and pace-setters of industrial policy, devising innovative growth strategies and delivering a rich array of services to the local economy. For others, more remarkable still is the fact that economic powers have been devolved in a setting marked by deep ideological divisions between the two major parties, and despite the strong presence of Communist administrations at local level. Most striking of all, however, is the connection between regional growth strategies and economic vitality in the "third Italy", the prosperous heartland of Italy's small-firm industrial districts. Stretching from the central Red Belt to the Christian Democratic stronghold in the north-east of the peninsula, these regions have witnessed the spectacular growth of a vast and vigorous economy of mini-manufacturing firms whose sophistication and dynamism on world markets is now a familiar story. Thus, whether run by the Communists (PCI) or Christian Democrats (DC), the regions at the centre of Italy's small business boom are the same regions that pioneer new schemes and provide extensive services for small industry.

In three ways, then, Italian regionalism seems to undermine the presuppositions commonly associated with arguments for centralism. First is the notion that in today's tightly integrated world economy, economic and industrial policies are matters that only the highest level of authority can cope with. Another is the expectation that in settings marked by strong political divisions, administrations of different ideological persuasions will necessarily use their autonomy to deviate from national policies. On both counts one need merely note, however, that in Italy, despite the post-war strength of the PCI

* Linda Weiss is a Lecturer in Sociology at Griffith University, Brisbane. She has published articles on Italian political economy and is the author of *Creating Capitalism: The State and Small Business Since 1945*, Oxford: Basil Blackwell, 1988.

in local government, the state has allowed a significant measure of decentralisation, and among regional administrations of different political persuasions one can now find considerable convergence on effective economic strategies.

Much more influential, however, is the claim currently fashionable among the radical liberal right. This is the well-known dogma that markets and politics are antithetical ways of organising society or, what amounts to the same point, that the expansion of the economy depends on a diminishing role for the state. Despite what one might expect, however, Italy's flourishing small firm economy—arguably the most prosperous and dynamic in the Western world—owes nothing to classical liberalism. On the contrary, it owes a great deal to an economic and social infrastructure whose foundations were laid by national governments and which is now being extended and managed in innovative ways by regional and local authorities. This conception of government-economy relations, I shall argue, provides a key to understanding the Italian experience.

My purpose is to shed some light on these apparently unexpected outcomes, concentrating on three tasks: How did the regions acquire such extensive economic powers? How important are regional strategies for the success of the small firm economy? What accounts for the continuity of policy objectives among ideologically diverse administrations? The discussion concentrates largely on the regions of the third Italy and examines their economic role in relation to one of the most spectacular developments of the post-war period: the consolidation of a decentralised system of craft-based industry, nowadays referred to as a regime of "flexible specialisation".

The underlying argument is somewhat paradoxical. Decentralist trends have been frequently attributed to failure or weaknesses of the centre, to some sort of inability to respond to increasing demands for socio-economic intervention. This paper takes a different tack. It suggests that the devolution of economic management to the regions owes much to the strength and success of the centre's policies whose core features, in this context, consist in the provision of a vast infrastructure for small industry. By strengthening a decentralised system of production, this gave some structural basis to the demands for a more decentralised form of economic management. And by emphasising the individual benefits of collaboration and collective provisioning, it also paved the way for an increasing convergence of policy interests between national and local political elites. It is time to pursue these themes in more detail.

Devolving Economic Powers: The Success of State Infrastructure

Our first task is to make sense of the novelty noted earlier: the extensive participation of regional governments in economic policy-making.

Today the regions plan and manage a range of policies which stretch right across the more "traditional" sphere of social services and territorial planning to embrace economic development as well. Whether in the sphere of production and finance, or in the labour and product markets, sub-national authorities have assumed an active and innovatory role in the development of their territorial economies. As others have commented, in unitary systems like Italy, such responsibilities have normally been reserved exclusively for the state.[1]

How was it possible for the regions to acquire such responsibilities? It must be stressed that in tackling that question, my chief concern is not to provide a full-blown account of regional reforms but to challenge the notion that state failure is somehow the heart of the matter and to offer a preliminary assessment of the region's economic role. We must look then to the contribution made by central policies and how these inadvertently laid the foundation for regional devolution. Thus the key issue is not why regional governments were created in the first place (or why they took so long in the making), but why the reforms were so extensive.

In clarifying this distinction, two points are in order. First, the desire and demand for a decentralised system of government did not suddenly spring to life as Italy entered an era of economic uncertainty in the 1970s. In repudiating the centralism of the Fascist period, the founding fathers of the Italian Republic, although divided on the type of regions to create, made clear provision for their establishment in the 1947 Constitution. But the vicissitudes of the Cold War and the Communists' exclusion from office served to push the moment of their enactment into the far distant future.[2] Despite their initial enthusiasm for decentralised government, the regnant Christian Democrats were reluctant to implement reforms which would undoubtedly strengthen an entrenched opposition in the periphery. What the DC feared above all was that the Left, already dominant in the central Red Belt, might use its powers to undermine national policies.

Once the Socialists were admitted into the governing coalition in 1962–3, however, it was perhaps only a matter of time before the Constitutional promise became a reality. Regional reforms, in short, became a price of their participation. Thus, despite many more years of foot-dragging on the part of the DC, the legislative machinery began slowly but inexorably to grind into motion. By 1968, then, the regions were well and truly on the political agenda and two years later, the necessary legislation was passed. Thus, as many others have noted, the

---

[1] M. Hebbert and H. Machin, *Regionalisation in France, Italy and Spain*, London School of Economics, London, 1984.

[2] At issue here is the creation of Italy's 15 *ordinary* regions, the source of all the foot-dragging. Italy's five Special Regions, consisting of the islands, Sardinia and Sicily, and three areas on the northern frontiers with mixed ethnic characteristics, were established mainly in the 1940s.

history of devolution in Italy tells a tale of an unfinished agenda brought
to conclusion—against deep misgivings and great reluctance in government circles—by the logic of the centre-left.[3]

This brings us to the second point. For there was nothing in that logic
which dictated the character that regionalism would ultimately take.
When they finally opened for business in 1972, it was clear that the
regions were little more than "super-provinces", administering the
decisions made at the centre and with few powers of any import.
Financial allocations illustrate the puny status of these fledgling
authorities: budgetary projections for 1975 anticipated an increase of
expenditures by the central bureaucracy of 20 per cent, as against a
mere 0.5 per cent for the regions.[4] But the story does not end there. In
1977–78 a full-fledged devolution of powers was carried out and it is
here that we enter the realm not merely of novelty, but of surprise. For
the new policy-making powers devolved to the regions went well beyond
those areas stipulated in the Constitutional provisions.

This is what deserves closer investigation. What may have led central
government to relinquish its monopoly in the economic-industrial
sphere? One of the most influential interpretations—both inside and
outside Italy—turns on the failures of central policies, weaknesses
ostensibly occasioned or exacerbated by the economic crisis of the
1970s. Such a conception certainly fits well with the prevailing
perception of the Italian state, best known for its sprawling bureaucracy
and paralysing inefficiency. It is an image that has earned notoriety well
beyond the shores of that country. Consider, for example, the
presumption of The Hudson Report that

> Even Italy . . . suffers mainly from a political ineptitude that, in its effect
> upon the society as a whole, is rather less important than ineptitude in
> Britain's leadership. The Italian state, as such, is in important respects
> irrelevant to what happens in Italian society.[5]

Like all good caricatures, this one does contain a strong kernel of
truth. But there are at least three reasons for doubting its explanatory
value. First, although grossly inefficient in some sectors of intervention,
such as the provision of social services, in other areas subsequently devoted
to the regions, such as small business development, state policies have
been outstandingly effective. And although many commentators have
lamented the shortcomings of Southern development policy, even here

---

[3] Peter Gourevitch, "Reforming the Napoleonic State: The Creation of Regional
Governments in France and Italy", in Sidney Tarrow, Peter J. Katzenstein and Luigi
Graziano (eds), *Territorial Politics in Industrial Nations*, Praeger, New York, 1977, p. 54.
[4] R. Leonardi, R. Y. Nanetti and R. D. Putnam, "Devolution as a Political Process",
Publius, Winter, 1981, p. 103.
[5] "The Wasting of Assets" in David Coates and John Hillard (eds), *The Economic
Decline of Modern Britain*, Wheatsheaf, Brighton, 1986, p. 143.

the record now shows a modest degree of success.[6] It is therefore highly misleading to generalise for all policy areas. For while some states are better than others at some things, it is equally true that all states are better at some things than others.

Another reason for doubting the "state failure" argument is that during the period prior to the extension of regional reforms, many municipalities were suffering severe problems of deficit financing. Whereas this may have led either to increasing centralism, as in Britain, or to a greater decentralisation of fiscal responsibilities, the response of the Italian state was simply to bail out its debt-ridden cities while maintaining control of the purse strings.

One final objection can be raised in this matter. If there is any substance to the "devolution by default" argument, then one would expect to find that the regions which pressed for a more advanced form of decentralisation were those suffering most from the centre's inadequacies. On the contrary, however, the regions most active and vociferous in that campaign were not the economic laggards, but the most prosperous regions like Lombardy, Tuscany and Emilia Romagna.[7]

These observations pave the way for a different explanation, one which draws on the success of state policies. As we will shortly see, the latter contributed to a more advanced form of regionalism by strengthening that area of the economy in which Italian production excels—small industry and crafts—above all in the regions of the Third Italy.

National policies: economic consequences

We begin with the economic consequences. These can be highlighted by noting that in the 1980s, Italy remains unusually blessed with small firms and that nowhere in the industrialised West has the economic vitality of small industry been more pronounced. While industrial concentration has been the norm in Europe and the United States for the post-war period as a whole, in Italy small-scale production has become increasingly prominent. By the 1970s, firms employing fewer than 100 personnel engaged 54 per cent of the industrial workforce, a share two to three times greater than in any other major industrial power (Japan being the one exception). By the 1980s, the trend to smallness was even more pronounced, the number of industrial firms rising by 40 per cent, and the average number of employees falling from 10 to 7.9. Today, in manufacturing industry alone, around 5 in every 10 employees work in firms with fewer than 50 personnel.

Thus, in defiance of all expectations about the relationship between industrial structure and economic performance, Italy is now the world's

[6] R. Cagliozzi, "A Regional or a National Industrial Policy?", *Review of Economic Conditions in Italy*, 1, 1982.

[7] R. Leonardi *et al.*, *op. cit.* p. 97.

fifth largest industrial capitalist power. Despite its recent agricultural beginnings and the perennial Southern question, Italy has more than doubled its share of manufacturing exports since 1945, and maintained higher rates of growth and lower rates of unemployment than the rest of the EEC as a group. And although it is burdened with a much more rapidly growing labour force than other European countries, Italian industry has nevertheless sustained a higher than average job-creation record. According to OECD figures, whereas industrial employment between 1973 and 1985 remained virtually flat in the rest of Europe, in Italy it rose by 6.5 per cent. As the Census and survey figures show, small companies in the Third Italy have been the main source of job-creation.

The importance of small industry to the Italian economy is well established not only in the macro indicators of economic performance, but also in the daily success stories of Italian producers clustered in the towns and provinces of central and north east Italy. The textile town of Prato, the knitwear district of Carpi, the engineering conglomerations in Modena and Reggio Emilia, the centre of musical instruments in Ancona and the furniture districts of Venetia are but some of the more favoured examples of Italian dynamism at home and abroad. They stand as symbols for the Third Italy: prosperous centres of sophisticated manufacturing industry where large firms are relatively few; regional economies based on complex systems of specialist producers.

Thanks to a number of excellent studies we now know much more about the sources of this extraordinary vitality. One, highlighted by Piore and Sabel,[8] stems from the technical virtuosity of the craft principles typically deployed by small Italian firms (for which Sabel has coined the term "flexible specialisation"). By matching multi-purpose machinery to skilled workers to turn out a wide range of specialist goods, flexible producers gain the edge over their mass-production counterparts in the ability to continuously reshape the production process. Another factor conducive to constant innovation and flexibility stems from the collaborative nature of production both within and between firms, attributed by some to the persistence of extended familial arrangements, by others to a rich network of public and private institutions (trade associations and political organisations) which promote co-operative behaviour.[9]

The importance of flexibility and social co-operation cannot be underestimated. But it is a fair bet that these features would not have much import today without the productive structures to sustain them, or—what amounts to the same point—if the Italian state had pursued the policies of its European and American counterparts since the end of

[8] Michael J. Piore and Charles F. Sabel, *The Second Industrial Divide: Possibilities for Prosperity*, Basic Books, New York, 1984.

[9] Arnaldo Bagnasco and Carlo Trigilia (eds), *Società e politica nelle aree di piccola Impresa: Il caso di Bassano*, Arsenale Editrice, Venezia, 1984.

the last war. Herein, as the comparative record suggests, lies the critical difference. Compared with the industrial strategies pursued in Europe throughout the postwar period as a whole (i.e. excluding more recent trends), Italian policies have exhibited an unusual degree of preference for the small firm. While most states for most of the time have promoted mergers, mass production and industrial concentration, Italian governments have shown far more reluctance to follow the big business track.[10]

A survey of all the major laws on incentives to industry throughout the post-war period, reveals a copious legislation of support, all privileging firms of small dimensions and most of which was initiated in the 1950s. Although the programmes are too numerous to detail, one can mention here some of the more important schemes created long before the advent of the regions. Among these, the Artisan Act deserves special mention. In 1956, the Italian state constructed a special category of small business designated as "artisan enterprise". In Italian law, the latter is defined not by the owner's qualifications or the nature of the product but by the size of a firm's workforce (for manufacturing firms, a maximum of 18–22 employees, depending on the number of apprentices involved). Firms so classified are entitled to a rich array of benefits. Since its inception artisan firms have enjoyed reduced tax and employers' contributions, special exemptions from certain property taxes, protection against bankruptcy proceedings, and a generous health and pension scheme subsidised by the state. In addition to the concessions which lower labour and running costs and provide welfare protection, post-war governments have also sponsored schemes for collective endeavours such as trade associations, industrial cooperatives and consortiums of small producers. Whether to bulk buy raw materials, to handle marketing and administration, to secure guaranteed loans or to share common facilities, small firms participating in these ventures are offered loan and export subsidies, infrastructure and preferential tax treatment. Little wonder, then, that in the 1980s artisan enterprise is the most favoured organisational form in the Italian economy!

Other examples of the success of national policies could be added; for instance the credit package financed under the Sabatini laws, which enables small engineering firms to purchase their equipment from Italian tool-makers. Today, Italy's highly dispersed machine tool industry is the second largest in Europe.

Finally, one must also note the immensely important financial infrastructure designed specifically for smaller enterprise. Artisans, for example, have their own permanent loan fund, financed, subsidised and guaranteed by the state, yet run independently of the central bureaucracy. In the first 23 years of its existence, the Artisan Fund assisted 300,000 firms with cheap loans. These covered 64 per cent of artisanal

---

[10] Much of this section draws on findings reported in Linda Weiss, *Creating Capitalism: The State and Small Business since 1945*, Basil Blackwell, Oxford and New York, 1988.

investment requirements and accounted for 75 per cent of new artisan firms established between 1953 and 1971.

In the aggregate, these results clearly illustrate the success of post-war policies initiated by the Christian Democrats. But a more territorially differentiated analysis can bring that point more sharply into focus. For if we ask which regions fared best from the various loan schemes for small industry over the twenty year period, 1956–1976, then the regions of the Third Italy emerge with a clear advantage. On virtually every indicator (e.g. number and amount of loans per firm), small firms in these regions captured the lion's share of low cost finance.

From the discussion thus far, we can see that the main impact of central policies has been to consolidate a decentralised productive system in which particular combinations of firms are preferred. This had two consequences for the transfer of economic powers to the regions. The first was structural. The more small specialist producers attracted others into their orbit, the more densely they clustered in industrial districts whose need for highly differentiated services could be most effectively met at local level. Thus the basis was laid for a more territorially differentiated development strategy. One further effect of these policies was thus to lend some material clout to the regions' claims for a more decentralised system of economic management. Hence, in the first phase of devolution (1970–1977), the demands for greater autonomy in promoting goods and services typical of a given region become increasingly insistent.

National policies: political consequences

It may be suggested, however, that none of these pressures on central government would have carried much weight were it not for one crucial fact: namely, that the Communists were perceived as legitimate and efficient economic managers at local level. Most striking in this context is the role of Left administrations in the traditional red regions of Umbria, Tuscany and especially Emilia Romagna, in promoting small firms.

In one important respect, this too was an unanticipated outcome of the DC's long-term strategy to favour a decentralised productive structure. By the late 1950s, the PCI was forced to reckon with a large industrial and commercial middle class about to undergo rapid expansion in the country as a whole. It could therefore either retreat into a strictly working class shell, like the French, or adopt a broad alliance policy which included small business. In choosing the latter—a strategy which has not been devoid of tensions and contradictions—the PCI sought not only to win the support of the urban middle class, but also to demonstrate its validity as a national force, capable of responding to the challenges posed by rapid industrial development.

Despite tight political and financial controls imposed by the centre,

Communist-run municipalities quickly gained a reputation for efficient and innovative administration. In the most solidly red region, Emilia Romagna, local authorities used their resources on infrastructure, both to upgrade the quality of transport, housing and welfare services, and to assist small firms with their projects by constructing exhibition halls for artisan products, sponsoring trade fairs and providing workshop facilities at low cost rental. By controlling the industrialisation process in such a way as to favour the small industrial and commercial middle class and block the penetration of big capital, the Communists thus underwrote the DC's own policy objectives at national level.

The significance of this apparent "convergence" for regional devolution was twofold: it enhanced the legitimacy of the PCI at local level, especially among the small business community; and it eliminated one of the most important pretexts for centralism. Whereas the DC could once plausibly claim that giving independence to Communist adminis-trations would undermine national policies, by the late sixties this was no longer possible. Emilia and its capital, Bologna, had become exemplary models for the rest of Italy.

We have seen then two ways in which the success of national policies contributed to a more decentralised pattern of economic management. How have the regions responded to their newly won capacities? What difference, if any, have they made to their local economies? It is time to turn to these questions.

Outdoing the Centre

One point should be clear from the previous discussion. Regional policy is not the central chapter in the Italian success story of small enterprise, but it is the most recent, and increasingly vital, one. As this implies, the regions—whether run by the Communists or Christian Democrats—have not used their power to "deviate" from national policies. Regional growth strategies, particularly in the centre-north, aim to promote small-scale production. To this extent, it can be said that they "converge" with the general goals of post-war legislation. It must be stressed, however, that this does not imply the absence of initiative or innovation at regional level. But insofar as the regions "do their own thing", the result is to improve upon, rather than deviate from, the programmes once controlled at the centre. Before probing the reasons for that convergence, let us first examine what the regions of the Third Italy are doing.

It would be an enormous task to survey the range of economic programmes undertaken by the various regions. Instead I focus on some of the more typical and important schemes currently on offer. These can be grouped into two main areas. The first, aimed at enhancing the *productive* potential of industrial districts, includes initiatives to encourage entrepreneurship, investment and innovation. The second seeks to expand the *marketing* opportunities of individual firms and regionally typical products and services.

Production policies: entrepreneurship, investment, innovation

By way of encouraging investment, innovation and entrepreneurship, the regions have taken the initiative in four integrated areas: financial services, industrial parks, research institutes, and vocational and retraining schemes. On the financial front, the major innovation has been the creation of regional development banks, credit-granting agencies whose chief task is to extend finance to small and medium-sized industry in the form of loan guarantees. As well as encouraging banks to lend capital to firms lacking collateral, these agencies provide industrial districts with a range of advanced services, including the training of management and technical staff, equipment rentals and computer services.[11]

Nevertheless, the main source of investment finance is still the subsidised credit directed to craft industry by the central government. While the latter remains the chief provider of these resources, it is the regions who now control their allocation. As a result, regional authorities have been able to introduce innovations of their own. Thus, for some purposes, they may encourage particular types of firms (such as co-operatives), or industries of special importance to the region. In other cases, they may stipulate certain conditions, such as the observation of social legislation and collective bargaining agreements, which firms must meet in order to receive loans.

Another major form of assistance to small industry is the preparation and servicing of industrial estates in which tens of hundreds of artisans engaged in complementary aspects of the same trade can rent space and share overheads and low-cost facilities. Launched by central government in the sixties in order to promote co-operation and joint action, the industrial estate programme took off under regional management. Together with the municipality, the region runs the consortia which prepare and service the industrial parks. By encouraging small firms to group together to share facilities and to provide each other with orders, the co-operative form of industrial estate combines the advantages of decentralised flexible production with the economies of centralised service provision.

To stimulate the technical innovations on which flexible specialists depend, several regions have begun to fill an important gap with the establishment of institutes for applied research. Mandated to specialise in one of three areas—the improvement of process technologies,

---

[11] The following discussion of regional programmes is based largely on information provided in Raffaella Y. Nanetti, *Growth and Territorial Policies: The Italian Model of Social Capitalism*, Pinter Publishers, London and New York, 1988; and S. Cassese, "Italy: a System in Search of an Equilibrium", in Hebbert and Mechin *op. cit.*

product design, or marketing and management systems—these institutes typically involve the co-operation and financial participation of the regions, local government, business organisations and, in certain cases, the universities. Examples of regional centres which lend technical assistance to specific industries include the Ceramic Centre in Emilia Romagna and the Electronic Institute for Industrial Quality in the Marche which conducts research on quality musical instruments.

No less important than any of these measures is the fourth major feature of regional infrastructure which supports innovation and entrepreneurship. The programmes in question here concern vocational education in the broadest sense, ranging from apprenticeship programmes to worker-retraining schemes and youth co-operatives. Since inheriting the state-supported apprenticeship programmes in 1972, the regions have devised novel strategies in response to the challenge of industrial restructuring and youth unemployment.

Most of the regions now run agencies which monitor the local labour market. Some regions have gone much further, working in close co-operation with business groups to plan, finance and implement vocational schemes which service the changing needs of industrial districts. In Emilia Romagna, for instance, the Centre of Vocational Education located in the city of Modena, in conjunction with the business community, identifies the new skills demanded by changing production processes—such as the application of computer graphics to colour pattern designs for fabrics—and carries out the necessary worker-retraining schemes. Several other regions promote entrepreneurial skills and alleviate the problem of youth unemployment at the same time by sponsoring co-operative enterprises.

Marketing policies: exhibitions and exports

Complementary to these production-centred initiatives are the programmes which enhance the commercialisation of the region's products and services generally and the marketing prospects of small firms in particular.

Among the various schemes on offer here, the most important concerns the creation of export consortia representing small and medium-sized firms in a particular industry. Initiated by central government in the sixties to stimulate the presence of small firms in foreign markets, the scheme encourages the formation of consortia with export subsidies and tax advantages. Since the 1970s, however, regional governments in the north and centre have entered the field with a plethora of promotional activities. Together with trade associations, the regions finance commercial missions, organise international fairs, undertake market analyses and assist in the final marketing of the product overseas.

As to the success of these initiatives, the strength of Italian small industry in foreign markets leaves no doubt. A more direct indication of their effectiveness comes from recent survey results which showed that firms participating in export consortia boosted their sales by 60 per cent in the four year period, 1979–83.

From this rapid survey, two key features of regional policy stand out. The first is an emphasis on extending the social infrastructure to meet the needs of small-firm industrial districts. In other words, regional initiatives embrace both market and welfare considerations: on the one hand, measures which aim to encourage new undertakings, improve the competitiveness of existing firms and stimulate the region's industry; on the other hand, programmes that aim to improve employment prospects via apprenticeship, retraining and youth co-operative schemes. But if these alleviate unemployment, they also replenish the pool of skilled labour and entrepreneurial talent necessary to a regime of permanent innovation. It is therefore difficult to identify in such a system where market strategies end and social "welfare" measures begin, since "welfare" is aimed at putting people into the job market, and the "market" is sustained by a social infrastructure.

The other major feature of regional programmes is the way they privilege collaboration and collective endeavours. By sponsoring industrial parks and export consortia, the regions enable small producers to reap the advantages of collective arrangements; and by running retraining and vocational schemes with the assistance of local employers and trade unions, they ensure a constant supply of skilled labour and entrepreneurial experience. Whether mobilising business organisations and trade unions to participate in the planning and administration of public services, or encouraging small producers to pool their efforts, it is hard to escape the conclusion that regional initiatives embody important "collectivist" elements—an anathema to free market thinking.

On both counts, that of social infrastructure and that of co-operation, the regions nicely meet the requirements of a regime of flexible specialisation and in these terms their policies must be judged a success. In the ten years since the regions acquired greater economic resources and responsibilities, the industrial districts of the north-east and centre have maintained high rates of growth, achieved an impressive job creation record and export performance, raised the level of technological sophistication of small industry, and increased per capita wages and productivity at rates well above the national average.

But the success of regional policy should not surprise us. There are, after all, important precedents for most of their programmes in the post-war policies pursued by the state. It would therefore be highly misleading to conclude that the regions have achieved what the state could not. Nevertheless, there are at least two areas where the regions are proving themselves more effective than the centre.

The first is their ability to police standards in the small firm sector, in collaboration with trade unions and employers. Although not yet widely practised outside areas controlled by the Left, such as Emilia, it appears that trade unions are increasingly encouraged by small employer organisations to police wage rates and supervise health and safety standards.

If this seems at odds with the prevailing stereotype according to which the small firm competes on wage and price cutting, it is precisely because flexible specialists must avoid that sort of competition. Piore and Sabel explain it thus. Small employers as a group are keen to discourage competition between firms in the form of wage and price reductions because this lowers quality standards by forcing everyone to do likewise. But by bringing in trade unions and by making "sweating" difficult, this encourages individual firms to compete through innovation rather than through labour exploitation. Because of the obvious benefits for the industrial district as a whole, small employers therefore have an interest as a group in observing working conditions and setting wage standards with trade unions, even when their employees are not members of such organisations.[12] Thus, to the extent that the regions encourage the presence of trade unions, this adds one more spur to the innovation process.

Where the regions also have the edge over the centre is in the ability to monitor and regulate local labour markets and to do so effectively by developing bilateral (trade union-region) and trilateral (trade union-region-business) relationships which mobilise the resources of the main social partners. Consequently, the regions are able to respond rapidly to the continuously changing patterns of demand, which call for new skills and technologies in the industrial districts.

On balance, then, it would appear that under regional management, small industry has gained even more advantages than under centralism. But that conclusion should not blind us to the much larger point that comes out of this discussion, namely, that the regions have been very busy *improving* upon, rather than deviating from, central policies. What accounts for this continuity of regional and national interests in support of small business development? Why, in particular, have Communist administrations continued to pursue a strategy which, to the labour Left outside Italy, seems inimical to the advancement of workers' interests?

Regions and the State: Convergence and Autonomy

The obvious response to the "convergence" puzzle is to argue that the regions are simply acting out an agenda established elsewhere, that the centre has all along been pulling the strings. How decentralised, then, is economic decision-making in Italy?

[12] Michael J. Piore and Charles F. Sabel, "Italian Small Business Development: Lessons for U.S. Industrial Policy" in J. Zysman and L. Tyson (eds), *American Industry in International Competition*, Cornell University Press, Ithaca, NY, 1983, pp. 409–10.

If federated nation-states like West Germany and the United States are our standard, then Italian devolution falls somewhat short of that model. The central government still has the deciding role in matters of foreign trade, credit and prices, as well as fiscal and public spending policies. Although the regions have wide spending autonomy, they rely for almost 90 per cent of their income on transfers from the state. Nor do the fifteen ordinary regions have any exclusive legislative powers. Rather, major regional legislation must conform with general guidelines elaborated in parliamentary framework laws which establish the boundaries on a given issue.

Yet the reality is rather more complex than the existence of these formal controls would suggest. Indeed, in many areas the necessary framework laws are non-existent. Moreover, once the regions had acquired a strong or over-riding interest in so many areas of socio-economic intervention, it became increasingly difficult to demarcate clear lines of responsibility between the various levels of government. Thus, for example, if the region was to control artisan industry, it also had to have powers to co-ordinate with those of central government in matters of trade and finance affecting that industry. Similarly, if it was to assume responsibility for vocational training, then it would also have to play some part in managing the centre's programmes for industrial restructuring, and so on. The overall effect of devolution, then, has not been to endow regional governments with inviolable areas of self-determination, but rather to increase the fusion and intermingling of areas of competence. The state may continue to exercise pre-enactment control over regional legislation, but the regions in turn routinely participate in central policy formulation.

For this reason, political decentralisation in Italy is best characterised as a participatory model of centre-local relations, in which forms of co-operation and co-management are much easier to identify than clear divisions of exclusive responsibility. The most common organisational device to secure participation is the creation of joint government bodies and mixed committees, undertaking tasks for, and requiring the consensus of representatives from, both levels of government. Because of the broad sharing of responsibilities, the widespread participation of policy-making processes and the limited scope of exclusive responsibility for any level of government, many commentators have likened the Italian system of devolution to a species of "co-operative federalism". However one chooses to characterise this system, the important point is that the existence of a continuous process of power sharing, concertation and bargaining among central and regional agencies and officials does not lend itself to hard and fast conclusions about who is "ultimately" in control of specific policy decisions. Since regional authorities are themselves important agenda-shaping bodies, we cannot therefore attribute the convergence of national and regional policies to some assumed lack of autonomy on the part of the regions.

If central control is not the answer, what accounts, then, for the continuity of initiatives which, even in regions controlled by the Left, favour decentralised production? Two considerations seem important here. The first is that the PCI has for some time recognised what the Left elsewhere still remains reluctant to concede—that small-scale production is not equivalent to the sweatshop writ large, and that its promotion is not necessarily in conflict with labour's advancement. To this end, as we have seen, Communist-led administrations at regional and municipal level have worked to improve small-firm capacities, not only by upgrading the social and economic infrastructure, but also by encouraging employer-union co-operation in the process of constructing and managing it. Moreover, far from excluding a significant role for trade unionism, the small-firm system of flexible specialisation is reaping considerable advantages from it. Thus by supervising training in a sector which relies upon continuous production changes, the unions help control the infrastructure that makes innovation possible. And by policing wages and working conditions, they help maintain the standards which make innovation necessary. One could add of course that, insofar as it tends to trade off formal regulation of the workplace for greater participation in decision-making, and to benefit the industrial district as a whole rather than specific groups of workers within it, this small-firm variant of trade unionism differs considerably from that which prevails under a mass-production system.[13] But the key point to emphasise here is that its presence and impact do serve to underwrite the long-term political and economic investment that leftist authorities have made in small-scale production.

While this interpretation draws attention to the character and strategy of the PCI, the second points us towards the political economy of Christian Democracy. At issue here is the extent to which the latter's perception of government's relation to the economy is one broadly shared by that of its chief opposition. In this regard, it is clear that the DC have been far from reticent about the use of state power for socio-economic development. The significance of this point is neatly illustrated in the dramatic contrast between the co-operative industrial estates promoted in Italy and the enterprise zones encouraged in British policy. Whereas the latter starts from the premise that collective benefits flow from the market of individual efforts, the Italian alternative operates on the assumption that individual benefits result from the politics of collective endeavours. For while liberalism tends to confuse two meanings of state power[14]—on the one hand, something oppressive, despotic or constraining; on the other, the infrastructural capacity to

[13] Charles F. Sabel, "A Fighting Chance", *International Journal of Political Economy*, 17, 3, 1987, pp. 48–9.
[14] John A. Hall, "Classical Liberalism and the Modern State", *Daedalus* 6, 3, 1987, 95–118.

penetrate and tax society in order to provide services—Christian Democracy has been far more at home with the latter conception.

Thus, if convergence on successful economic policy has been possible to a greater degree in Italy than in Britain, this is primarily because opposing political forces have been divided least where it matters most. The choice between market or politics, in other words, has not been a divisive issue, and in this respect, at least, the Italians have more successfully avoided power standoffs than their British counterparts. Consequently, the question of centre-local relations (whether to provide a given service locally or centrally) has not, as seems to be the case for Britain, been subsumed under that much larger issue of government-economy relations (whether to provide a given service at all).

What conclusions can we draw from this analysis? Clearly, there is little in the nature of institutional arrangements themselves which ensures the success of economic policy. Small firms thrived under centralism. Today they are prospering under regionalism. This is not to deny the greater advantages for the smaller-firm sector, which a decentralised system of economic governance can provide. But to focus on policy differences between national and regional government is, I have argued, to look in the wrong place. In the light of the policies examined in these pages, it is the similarities, not the differences, which are the more striking and significant.

It is these similarities which force one to conclude that the spread and success of decentralised production are inseparable from the existence of a massive infrastructure in whose creation both the state and the regions have participated. But the significance of that infrastructure, so much at odds with neo-liberal thinking, goes well beyond its small firm consequences. For it is also at the root of the collaborative relations which have developed between central and sub-national authorities. To phrase the point in slightly different, somewhat bolder terms, if post-war governments had championed neo-liberal strategies, the PCI would very likely have conceived decentralised production as inimical to labour's interests and, in all likelihood, neither Italy's small firm "miracle" nor extensive economic devolution would have seen the light of day. Fortunately for Italy, then, the individualistic tenets of the radical right find little social resonance. How could they when the fruits of individual effort are so visibly the result of socially provided benefits? This, surely, is the most important lesson to be gained from the Italian experience of regionalism.

THE "FREE LOCAL GOVERNMENT" EXPERIMENTS AND THE PROGRAMME OF PUBLIC SERVICE REFORM IN SCANDINAVIA

JOHN STEWART AND GERRY STOKER*

THIS article focuses on the "free local government" experiments in Scandinavia which have given local authorities greater freedom to meet local needs and more opportunities for experimentation and initiative in the organisation and delivery of services. The experiments are part of a wider programme of reforms aimed at increasing the responsiveness and effectiveness of public services and intervention. The "free commune" initiative was launched in Sweden in 1984 as part of that wider programme and similar experiments followed in Denmark, Norway and Finland. Our main emphasis will be on the more developed Swedish scheme, but we will also comment on the initiatives of the other Scandinavian countries.

Before exploring the public service renewal programme and the place of the "free local government" experiment within it we shall provide some brief background information on the structure and functions of local government in Scandinavia and explore some of the key cultural underpinnings of the Scandinavian system. The piece ends with an assessment of the "free local government" experiment and of its implications for local government in this country. Its significance here is as an illustration of countries seeking to extend decentralisation and increase local autonomy. The experimental mode gives it a special interest since it recognises that decentralisation is not easily achieved. It is a process in which both central and local government have to learn.

It is never easy to compare the extent of local autonomy across countries. Many features of the Scandinavian system described here would suggest that Scandinavian authorities have greater autonomy than those in this country. Local authorities have a general competence and a strong basis in local government finance which distinguishes them from this country. On the other hand, many of the duties imposed on

* Institute of Local Government Studies, University of Birmingham. Professor John Stewart has published several books on local government, including *The New Management of Local Government*, Allen and Unwin (1986). Dr Gerry Stoker wrote *The Politics of Local Government*, Macmillan (1988) and was co-author with John Stewart of the Fabian Society pamphlet *From Local Administration to Community Government* (1988).

local authorities have traditionally been spelt out in a detail that contrasts with the broad powers and duties of British legislation. The apparent freedom given by local authority taxation can be limited formally or informally by agreements between local authority associations and the government. The extent of local authority autonomy cannot be simply measured, it has to be grounded in understanding of how a system works.

But if comparisons of local autonomy are not easily made, it is more straightforward to compare the direction in which systems are moving. The significance of the free local government experiments is that they represent a commitment to decentralisation at a time when in this country there is increasing centralisation.

Local Government Structures in Scandinavia[1]

All the Scandinavian countries with the exception of Finland have a two-tier system of local government with district or municipal authorities as the primary local government bodies and an upper tier of county authorities. During the post-war period the reform of local government boundaries has resulted in a reduction in the number of authorities and an increase in their population size. In Sweden there are 284 municipalities and 24 county councils providing for Sweden's 8.3 million inhabitants. Some of the municipalities serve large cities and others provide for the vast and sparsely populated rural areas of the country. Only 11 municipalities have populations of more than 100,000 and there are 66 municipalities with populations of less than 10,000. There is a similar diversity in the populations covered by the 24 counties. The county of Stockholm with about 1.6 million inhabitants is the largest and Gotland is the smallest with a population of about 56,000.

Norway has a similar two-tier system with 448 municipalities and 18 counties. Oslo, however, is not incorporated in any county and has a mixed status. The population covered by the authorities is on average smaller than in Sweden, with just over half of all municipalities having under 5,000 inhabitants. In Denmark there are 213 district authorities and 14 counties, with Copenhagen and Frederiksberg being city authorities with county status. Finland has only one tier of local authorities. It has 461 municipalities, divided between 84 urban and 377 rural authorities, a distinction that has become mainly symbolic as their powers have grown closer together.

---

[1] More detailed assessments of local government in two of the Scandinavian countries are provided in reports prepared by Alan Norton at the Institute of Local Government Studies. See A. Norton, *Notes on Local and Regional Government in Advanced Western Democracies: Sweden and Denmark*, INLOGOV, Birmingham, 1988.

Functions

All Scandinavian countries provide their local authorities with a power of "general competence". Local authorities, within the limits of the law, have a full discretion to undertake activities on behalf of their inhabitants. In addition individual statutes place a duty on local authorities to provide particular services.

Local authorities have developed a responsibility for a wide range of public expenditure and functions. In 1985 Swedish local government spent 22 per cent of GDP, and a similar proportion is spent in Norway. In both Finland and Denmark local authorities are major service providers. Throughout the post-war period the local government sector expanded considerably. The growth rate decelerated in the 1970s but local authorities have remained major institutions of the welfare state.

The split in the responsibilities held by upper and lower tier authorities varies. In Sweden the principal responsibilities of the two tiers is set out in Figure 1.

The lower tier municipal authorities have a broad responsibility for social environmental welfare. The key task of county councils is health

FIGURE 1 THE DIVISION OF RESPONSIBILITIES BETWEEN COUNTY COUNCILS AND MUNICIPAL AUTHORITIES IN SWEDEN

Type of authority	Responsibility
County Council	Medical care and health services: out-patient care, general hospitals, nursing homes, psychiatric hospitals, preventative (individual) health care, public dental service
	Care of mentally retarded (special schools)
	Social welfare: family counselling, children's homes
	Specialised training: nursing and care occupations, folk high schools
	Arts
	Commerce and Industry
	Vocational rehabilitation
	Local and Regional Communications
	Regional Planning
Municipalities	Social welfare, compulsory schooling (aged 7–16), pre-school activities (play schools, nurseries), housing, land, waste, environmental and health protection, emergency and fire services, leisure, sports, arts, streets, parks, planning, civil defence, electricity and water supply, energy planning, local and regional communications

Source: A. Gustafsson, Local Government in Sweden, The Swedish Institute, 1988, p. 40.

care. Health services and medical care consume about three quarters of total county council spending. There are a number of overlapping and shared responsibilities and there is an ongoing debate about the appropriate allocation of functions between tiers.

The core local services are mainly supplied directly by local authority departments. However, many utilities and other services are provided by fully or partly owned local authority companies (sometimes supported by a range of different local authorities). Some housing and other functions are undertaken by foundations or "non-profit" companies. The companies are legally separate from the local authorities and are generally expected to operate on a self-sustaining basis but it is common for all of the directors to be local authority appointees. In 1983 there were some 1300 such companies in which municipalities or county councils had controlling interests. Finally, local authorities can also set up formal joint federations to meet their shared responsibilities. In 1986 there were, however, only 19 such federations dealing with water supply, public transport, fire prevention and other matters. These federations are statutory bodies representing a permanent commitment to co-operation.

Finance

The key source of local revenue raising capacity in Scandinavia is the power available to municipalities and counties to set a local tax. In 1985 in Sweden the local tax which is levied mainly on income and to a limited extent on property covered, on average, about 41 per cent of municipal expenditure and 62 per cent of county council expenditure. In Norway, Finland and Denmark local income tax is the main source of revenue, but is supplemented by local property/land taxes. In Norway there is a limit to the level of local income tax and all authorities have reached that limit. In Denmark the Government recently proposed to limit local income tax for counties and districts, but only their proposals for counties gained a majority in Parliament.

Local authorities also receive grant support from national government in all Scandinavian countries. In Sweden these central government grants take a variety of forms. Some are paid to finance local government services in particular fields, e.g. medical care, education, child care. Central government grants in 1985 accounted for about 26 per cent of municipal revenue and 18 per cent of county revenue.

The remaining sources of revenue for local authorities in Sweden are charges for services, especially municipal utilities such as electricity, water etc., but also in some cases for day nursery and welfare facilities. Municipalities and county councils are also entitled to raise short-term or long-term loans primarily in order to finance capital expenditure.

LOCAL GOVERNMENT IN SCANDINAVIA

The structure of Scandinavian local government: some reflections

The main feature that the British observer sees in the Scandinavian systems is the relatively small size of the local authorities. For example, the average size of a district is 29,300 in Sweden and 18,600 in Denmark—far below the average sizes of district councils in Britain which in any event do not have the wide range of responsibilities of a Scandinavian authority. However, the readiness of Scandinavian local authorities to work in ways that do not follow the pattern traditional to this country of direct provision through local authority departments and instead to work through companies, foundations and joint action makes scale less critical.

The importance of the local income tax is that it gives local authorities a buoyant tax clearly related to ability to pay, which along with the principle of general competence expresses principles of local autonomy. There are of course limits. There are limits to the general competence and in Norway (and now for counties in Denmark) there are limits to the local income tax. But generally the power of general competence and a strong capacity for local revenue raising express a high commitment to local government.

The Political Culture for Local Government

To describe formal structures is not enough. Structures have to be understood in the cultures in which they are embedded. Three features of the Scandinavian and in particular the Swedish political culture are highlighted: the interactive process, the commitment to local autonomy and the bureaucratic tradition, for these influence the actual nature of local government and set the conditions for the free commune experiment.

The interactive process

The real problem in comparing the extent of local autonomy in Sweden and in this country is that in this country there is a separation between the world of local government and of the centre. In the public services the careers and training of civil servants and local government officers follow separate paths. In the political parties there is only limited interaction between councillors and Members of Parliament. There are two cultures: the culture of local government and the culture of central government. The Swedish political culture is not marked by the same divide. Agne Gustafsson quotes a Government Commission as characterising relations in the following terms: "The relationship between state and local authorities is no longer characterised by fundamentally different interests but by a common endeavour to promote the best interests of citizens, by constant shifts in the mutual division of labour, by continuous co-operation in a variety of forms and by mutual dependence".[2] Such words have been heard in this country, but in Sweden it expresses a dominant culture.

Local councillors play a greater role in the national parties than in this country. The institution of a common polling day for national and local elections in Sweden is an expression of the inter-relationship between national and local politics. The size and strength of the local authority associations is another indicator of the relationship. The associations have concluded agreements with the Government on local taxation and on other matters which they have recommended to their members.

The County Administrative Board is a further example of the inter-relationship. This is charged with certain central government functions and the co-ordination of national, county, and district functions in each county, of which the head is the County Governor appointed now by the Government, although formerly by the King, but the members of which are elected by the county council.

In an inter-active system it is hard to assess the real extent of local autonomy. Although local authorities control the local income tax, their use of that tax has been the subject of agreements between the local authority associations and central government, which local authorities have generally followed. The actual operation of an inter-active system is determined more by patterns of influence than by patterns of authority.

An ideology of local self-government

Agne Gustafsson argues: "Local self-government has long been one of the cornerstones of the Swedish Constitution. The decentralised decision-making which this has made possible has contributed greatly to the country's democratic, economic, social and cultural development".[3] The commitment to an ideology of local self-government has influenced action. Gustafsson concludes that, while there have been variations, there has been a consistent tendency for decentralisation from state to regional or local level, including the transfer to virtually all the districts of responsibility for schools up to and including upper secondary schools.

One factor, special to Sweden, that may assist the process of decentralisation is that, for central government, the choice in the allocation of responsibilities is not between local authorities and central government departments, but between state agencies and local authorities. The ministries themselves are very small, normally containing no more than 100 staff (including clerical staff). The ministries are concerned mainly with legislation and regulations and the policy issues that

[2] A. Gustafsson, *Local Government in Sweden*, The Swedish Institute, Stockholm, 1988, p. 62–4.
[3] *Ibid.*, p. 11.

underlie them. The Swedish local authority association employs far more staff than most ministries. There is a necessary degree of inter-dependence, but more important because of the commitment to local self-government, there is mutual respect. Within the interaction between central and local government, local government has considerable leverage.

A legalistic tradition

In assessing the degree of autonomy, regard has, however, also to be given to the legal tradition which gives a particular character to the working of local government and can reinforce bureaucratic tendencies. Although local authorities have a general competence, many of their activities are carried out in accordance with legislation and regulations which lay duties upon local authorities as opposed to giving powers they may exercise. The legislation and derived regulations are often written with a detail which contrasts with the broad terms in which much British legislation, at least until recently, was drafted.[4]

In addition, local authorities, like other public bodies, are subject to systems of appeal to ensure that they are acting within the law. As Elder has pointed out, writing more about central government and the national agencies than of local authorities: "Decentralisation is linked with the regulation of administrative activity by formal rules, and the individual responsibility of civil servants reinforces the importance of their knowing the legal ropes. Administrative coherence and consistency owe much to the elaborate system of administrative appeals".[5]

To a large extent public administration has long been seen as the application of legal rules. The institution of the position of the Ombudsman and the role of the Chancellor of Justice in interpreting administrative law as far back as the eighteenth century reinforce this concept.[6] The result has been that "the procedures of public authorities become pervaded by a formalism which was considered to be both a symbol of and a safeguard for the dispensing of even-handed justice from one case to the next. These traditional attitudes have become harder to maintain as the state has expanded its activities rapidly in the social and economic field".[7] Those traditions can lead to the Swedish system of administration at both local and central government level being over-bureaucratic. It can also mean that the commitment to local autonomy is set within what at times appears over-detailed regulation.

---

[4] On the changing nature of British legislation see M. Loughlin, *Local Government in the Modern State*, Sweet and Maxwell, London, 1986.

[5] N. Elder, *Government in Sweden*, Pergamon, Oxford, 1970, pp. 104–5.

[6] N. Elder, A. Thomas and D. Arter, *The Consensual Democracies? The Government and Politics of the Scandinavian States* (Revised Edition) Basil Blackwell, Oxford, 1988, pp. 138–143.

[7] N. Elder, 1970, *op. cit.*, p. 104.

That is the starting point for the "free commune" experiment, which is in part an escape from over-regulation inappropriate, as Elder points out, to present activities. The stress on local self-government means that a national programme for lessening bureaucratic controls is expressed through experiments in increased local autonomy.

We have concentrated in this section on Sweden, but many of the features of the Swedish system, with the exception of the special role of the ministries, are features of the other Scandinavian countries to a greater or less extent. The shared culture of what have been described as the consensual democracies is supported by close working relationships between governments and learning from each other, as the spread of the "free commune" experiment and the wider programme for public service renewal illustrates.

The Public Service Renewal Programme

The "free commune" experiments are part of a broader commitment to reform the public services, in which Sweden has led the way. Twin forces contributed to a growing concern with the nature of state provision in Sweden. First there was growing evidence during the 1970s of public disillusionment with the public sector which was seen as unresponsive and over-bureaucratic. Services were not close to the public as customer and failed to involve the public as citizens. Second, with a world-wide economic downturn there was concern about the level of public expenditure. After years of growth, financial restraint and manpower cutbacks were demanded, leading to a new stress on the need for efficiency.

The reaction of the Social Democratic Party, long dominant in Swedish politics, to these shifts in opinion and climate contrasts with that of the British Labour Party which took up a much more limited position in the late '70s and early '80s: defending jobs and services without realising that more than defence was required of services which were seen by many as having grown remote from those they served. The Social Democratic Party argued that to meet the new challenges what was required was not just a sustained commitment to public service and welfare objectives but a transformation of the nature of public service delivery and performance.

The Social Democrats had been continuously in power since 1932 but were defeated in 1976 when the three main centre and right parties formed a coalition. Towards the end of that period the scale of public provision came under attack from at least some of those parties. The Social Democrats came to terms with the realisation that a critique of the public services had popular support and returned to power in 1982 committed to a programme of public service renewal. Lennart Gustafsson, the Secretary of Planning in the Ministry of Public Administration responsible for the programme, has written that:

132

Basically the problems that the Government had to solve were as follows:

Economic resources were scantier than before. New problems could no longer be solved by committing additional resources. Reappraisals and streamlining measures were called for.

The gap between public agencies and the individual had widened, due to public organisation having become excessively complicated and unduly pre-occupied with technical considerations.

Public activities had excessively supplanted the active involvement of the citizen in solving individual or collective problems.

The public take an increasingly serious view of shortcomings in the service-mindedness of the authorities and in their capacity for dealing with the general public.[8]

The programme has the broad objectives of improving the efficiency and effectiveness of the public sector and developing public services that are responsive to the public as customer and as citizen. The commitment to the welfare state remains. As the Swedish Ministry of Public Administration puts it: "the objectives of the welfare state are to stand fast. It is the means to those ends which are being reconsidered".[9]

The renewal programme has four main elements: to increase consumer choice within public services; to strengthen democratic control over government; to improve efficiency and effectiveness; and to provide more responsive services.

Greater freedom of choice

In part this is being achieved by giving the public a greater opportunity for choice of schools, doctors and nurseries, but it is also being achieved by giving greater influence to users.

This is to be done by strengthening the position of users rather than by admitting private alternatives involving commercial interest. The most important thing, given this approach, is not for citizens to be given the opportunity of choosing between different alternative forms of child care, schooling, health care etc., but for activities to be organised exactly as the users want them to be—naturally subject to the restrictions dictated by the available resources and by insistence on fair and equal treatment.[10]

There are difficult issues involved in this extension of choice through user influence and control. There are political issues as to how far such choices by users can cut across the need for national standards. The emphasis has been on experiments and encouraging local initiatives.

[8] L. Gustafsson, "Renewal of the Public Sector in Sweden", *Public Administration*, vol. 65, No 2, 1987, pp. 179–80.
[9] The Swedish Ministry of Public Administration, *Information Note*, June 1988.
[10] L. Gustafsson, 1987, *op. cit.*, p. 180.

Stronger democratic control

A wide range of measures is being taken. The Government recognises that the re-organisation of local government increased both the organisational and geographical distance between local authorities and their citizens. They are therefore encouraging local authorities to devolve powers to local committees. Greater user influence is also seen as strengthening democratic control and the Government has been considering legislation based on the principle of "conditional delegation". This means that "decision-making powers are delegated to an employee at a municipal institution, on condition that he consults the clients affected before deciding a given question."[11]

The "free commune experiment" is part of this programme. By giving greater freedom to local authorities, local democratic control is being strengthened.

Greater efficiency and effectiveness

Much of this programme emphasises themes of value for money familiar in this country. The programme has, however, placed a special emphasis on changing the relationship between the small Swedish ministries and the government agencies. Emphasis is now to be placed on policy direction rather than detailed administrative and financial control. Experiments are being undertaken in co-ordinated administration at county level and decentralisation by the state agencies for effective management is being pursued. Local authorities are being encouraged to pursue similar policies for improving productivity.

The service programme

The Government places a special emphasis on the service programme: "The Government has emphasised the importance of an improved service afforded by the civil service and the service campaign which came into being bears the motto 'Less control and less bureaucracy' . . . It has become increasingly important to remind people that the public sector was primarily built up to serve the public".[12] The Government has realised that there is little that can be done by central government directly. Better and more responsible services can only be built close to the public. The stress has been on setting a climate for the service emphasis, encouraging experiments and above all the use of SIPU, the main personnel agency, as a catalyst for change through training and consultancy.

The themes of Sweden's reform programme for the public sector have

[11] *Ibid.*, p. 183.

[12] L. Jeding and B. Beckman, *The Public's View of the Public Sector*, SIPU, Stockholm, no date, p. 1.

been taken up by all parties and by other Scandinavian countries of differing political persuasions. While there may be political differences about the scale of public service, there is a general commitment to service renewal programmes. In Denmark in 1983 the then controlling non-socialist coalition launched a "modernisation programme" for the public sector with the aims of reducing detailed controls, improving management and extending customer choice and participation. Norway and Finland, too, have adopted many of the themes of the Swedish programme.

Although the renewal programme has the general approval of the other main political parties and of the trade unions in Sweden, it has taken longer to develop and have an impact than was hoped. Some point to a degree of reluctance among senior civil servants and key politicians to give sufficient impetus to the reforms. But, in addition, the nature of the reforms being attempted raise many difficult issues and are time-consuming. Problems include how to meet the political and ideological challenges raised by a commitment to consumer choice. How to provide choice where market allocation through price is not involved? To what extent should choice be allowed to undermine national standards? Should different ethnic groups or religious sects be allowed to determine the form of education received by their children? There are limits to which public services can be responsive to individual customers. Public services have many customers whose interests have to be reconciled. The requirements of government are not necessarily the same as the requirements of service.

As well as these political and ideological dilemmas, major changes in organisation behaviour and staff attitudes are required for the programme to work. Legislation and regulation—the traditional tools of national government—are less relevant. The programme is premised on creating a new climate of ideas, encouraging experimentation and developing new forms of management. Such changes are never easily achieved and will involve a long-term commitment. They require a changed approach from both central government and the direct service providers in the public sector.

The Free Local Government Experiments

The Swedish "Free Commune" experiment

The general background to the "free commune" experiment in Sweden has already been outlined. The experiment is seen as building on the tradition of local autonomy in Sweden and the potential of the large units of local government established in the period of reorganisation in the 1950s and '60s. The experiment is explicitly seen as part of the broader attempt to shift the pattern and nature of public service in Sweden. As a report from the Ministry of Public Administration argues:

135

This experiment in "greater local autonomy" . . . is not to be regarded as an isolated experiment involving a limited number of municipalities and county councils. Instead it is part of a much greater process of change relating to the control of Sweden's public sector and the apportionment of responsibilities there. It is a process historically rooted in traditional local autonomy, organisationally stemming from the municipal boundary reforms and politically prompted by a determination to improve local government activities, without pre-empting additional resources, and to deepen the quality of local democracy.[13]

The "free communes" experiment was launched in July 1984. Four goals were set for the initiative: to establish opportunities for testing new departures in municipal administration and county activity; to allow for increased adaptation of policy measures to local conditions; to increase the influence of individual members of the public over service delivery; and to augment local autonomy. As experiments they gave the Government and the local authorities the opportunity to learn from change carried out on a limited scale. Lessons learned could then be applied more widely, if necessary through national legislation.

A group of nine municipalities and three county councils were selected for the special status of a "free commune" under legislation providing for greater local accountability. These selected local authorities have been allowed to apply for exemptions from regulations issued by national authorities, from statutory instruments and in some cases from legislative provisions in order to pursue new forms of organisation, service delivery and intervention. The experiment was to continue until 31 December 1988. Initiatives in two fields—certain medical services and the organisation of municipal committees—have had their time-scale extended until 1991. And there is currently before the Riksdag legislation to extend the entire scheme to 1991 and bring in additional municipal and county participants.

Certain restrictions were imposed on the scheme. Exemptions were not to be awarded for experiments neglecting certain "fundamental" considerations such as: the fair distribution of social services; the protection of the lives and health of the public; the protection of particularly disadvantaged groups; legal safeguards; the general economy. These restrictions show that the Social Democrats were unwilling to see basic objectives of welfare and equality challenged. Greater local autonomy was being allowed within a framework of national priorities. Beyond this, however, the Minister of Public Administration called for "a bold, innovative approach".[14]

A system for monitoring the progress of the experiment in the various

[13] The Swedish Ministry of Public Administration, *Free Local Government Experiment in Sweden* (Report compiled by Gunnar Johnson). Paper presented to Council of Europe Conference on "Free Local Government: Deregulation, Efficiency and Democracy", Ostersund, Sweden, 28–30 June 1988, p. 8.

[14] Quoted in *ibid.*, p. 11.

"free communes" was established. A National and Local Government Advisory Committee—consisting of representatives of the ministries mainly affected by the experiment together with representatives of the national associations of municipalities and county councils—has been charged with acting as a communication point for the "free communes" and ensuring that the experiment is systematically and comprehensively evaluated. The local authorities included in the experiment reflect the diverse nature of Swedish local government. They are spread throughout the country and have a variety of demographic, economic and political characteristics.

By mid-1988, 284 different proposals concerning exemptions and other measures had been put forward by the "free communes". On average the number of proposals from the county councils was smaller than that from the municipalities. This is probably explained, however, by the fact that the paramount activity of the county councils—health and medical services—is governed by a recent paving Act which gives the councils considerable freedom of action. In addition, other legislative changes in particular policy areas (e.g. care of the mentally retarded) have provided county councils with opportunities for experimentation.

About 20 per cent of the proposals put forward by the local authorities were rejected by central government. They were considered to neglect legal safeguards, to involve too great an increase in public expenditure or to fall outside the scope of the experiment. A third of the proposals gave local authorities the right to experiment outside the constraints of general legal controls and provisions. A quarter of the proposals led to general changes in rules or regulations in order to allow them to proceed, while in the case of just over 15 per cent of the submissions it was found that the proposed changes could go ahead without any alteration to the rules.

A range of policy areas has attracted the attention of the "free communes". Over 20 per cent of proposals related to the planning and development sector. Indeed many of the proposed exemptions in this area were subsequently incorporated in a new Planning and Building Act. About 25 per cent of proposals related to the operation and running of schools. Some 11 per cent involved local authority activity in the labour market and in economic development. Nearly 14 per cent involved experiments in health and social welfare. Other areas in which experiments have developed include environmental protection, transport, housing and the organisation of local authorities. In the last category new committee structures have been established, with in some cases area-based political organisation replacing the traditional functional or service based committees.

The proposed changes vary a great deal in significance. Some have quite large-scale consequences but others are more small-scale and limited in their impact. In order to give a flavour of the type of initiatives involved we conclude this discussion with an examination of the experience of two areas visited by one of the authors.[15]

The Municipality of Bracke is situated in the County of Jamtland in the middle of Sweden. It is a predominantly rural area with a number of scattered villages and towns and a total population of about 6,000 residents. As a "free commune" Bracke has experimented with the funding and staffing of its schools and social services. It has undertaken a range of job creation initiatives and set up mechanisms to support local farming, forestry and fishing interests. It has also experimented with a system of area-based committees to manage its affairs, while at the same time establishing a number of local authority-owned companies to run particular services.

Ostersund is also a municipality in the County of Jamtland. It is the main administrative centre in the area with a population of about 60,000. Jamtland, as a "free county council", has launched an experiment in joint care with the municipality. In Sweden, as noted earlier, the county councils are responsible for public health and medical care while the municipalities run most social welfare. This division creates problems requiring close co-operation if they are to be adequately resolved. The Brunflo experiment in Ostersund establishes a unique joint local care organisation overseen by a local political executive appointed by the county council and the municipality. The local centre provides in one location a combined range of health and social welfare services. The aim of the experiment is to test this method of developing welfare state provision in order to provide a more integrated service and better continuity in care.

Developments in other Scandinavian countries

Free local government experiments have also been developed in Norway and Denmark and in the beginning of 1989 the first phase of a similar initiative will be started in Finland.[16]

The Norwegian free local government experiment was launched in May 1986 and by the end of that year 20 municipalities and four counties had been granted special status.[17] The special status local authorities can receive exemptions from laws and regulations about how tasks are to be solved and activities organised. In addition, they can determine their own by-laws and put them forward for approval by the national government.

During 1987 and the early part of 1988 much effort and time has gone

[15] These study visits were organised as part of the Council of Europe Conference on "Free Local Government: Deregulation, Efficiency and Democracy".

[16] Information on the Finnish initiative was obtained from Mr Kari Prattala, Deputy Head of Legal Department, Finnish Municipal Association.

[17] Association of Local Authorities, *Free Local Government in Norway—a Pilot Project*. Paper presented at the Council of Europe Conference, 28–30 June 1988.

into framing by-laws and developing the detailed plans for experimental projects. By mid-1988 nearly two dozen by-laws had been approved and over 50 projects established. Work has taken place in five main areas, paralleling to a large extent the experience of Sweden. The five areas are: industrial and economic development, new forms of youth and school provision, co-ordination between health and social service sectors, simplification of land-use zones, planning and building regulations, and the restructuring of municipal organisation with the twin objectives of increased political influence and improved administrative efficiency. A major research-based evaluation of the free local government experiment is being undertaken.

In Denmark a free local government experiment was initiated in 1985.[18] It includes six regional or county authorities and 30 municipal authorities which are allowed to apply for exemption from general rules applying to local government. By mid-1988 a total of 545 projects had been put forward by the free local authorities. About a third have been approved and are being implemented. But a third have been refused or withdrawn by the local authorities on the expectation of the project being rejected. The final third are still in the pipe line. A research study found varying attitudes among different government departments to the experiment. In the school, leisure, and cultural field about 45 per cent of projects were approved, while the percentage of approvals was only 20 per cent in the social and health area. The subjects of the initiatives are similar to those developed in Sweden and Norway. Forty per cent were concerned with school management and leisure education, 27 per cent with planning and land-use matters, and the remainder focused on employment, social and health arrangements, budgetary and accountancy rules, the organisation of local authorities, tax arrangements and energy conservation.

Some specific examples give the flavour of the initiatives in Denmark. The local authority of Herlev has experimented with devolving its powers of local committees in two neighbourhood areas. North Jutland County has pursued economic development and employment creation activities which are normally specifically outside the remit of local authorities; while 12 local district authorities have taken over responsibility for granting permission to develop land from their county councils.

An Assessment of the Free Local Government Experiments

It is clear that the different initiatives stimulated by the "free" status of selected local authorities have a variable impact on the system of government. Some involve fairly small-scale changes but others involve a major transfer of responsibilities or new organisational forms.

[18] Association of County Councils, *Free Local Government in Denmark*. Paper presented at the Council of Europe Conference, 28–30 June 1988.

All the national governments have shown some caution about the schemes they are prepared to sanction. Indeed one Danish local government observer has complained "even if ministers have been positive, the obstruction and open resistance in central administration has often turned the approval of an experiment into a bureaucratic *tour de force* of Kafkaesque dimension".[19] In some instances the local authorities themselves have been uncertain about taking on new responsibilities without increased resources. Further, despite the emphasis given to citizen participation and involvement it is the case that much of the experimentation has been developed by authorities without community involvement. In addition, many of the changes have little direct impact on individual members of the public. Most of the changes involve a redistribution of responsibilities and power among politicians and officials rather than to the citizenry, although other parts of the renewal programme have given greater emphasis to involvement by the public as customers or citizens.

Above and beyond the achievement of particular projects in improving the efficiency and effectiveness of service delivery, the Scandinavian "free local government" experiments have contributed to a broad programme of change within their public sectors. In the first place, the experience of learning by experiment has proved useful. Instead of arriving at final solutions by means of official inquiries or government committees the strategy has been to gain experience through experimentation before making general policy decisions. Both national governments and local authorities have found this a valuable way of proceeding. Secondly, the establishment of "free communes" has helped to develop an ethos of re-thinking and questioning. As the Swedish Ministry of Public Administration argues: "new ideas have been hatched, ideas which would not probably have emerged without a positive climate of change".[20] Or in the words of Denmark's Association of County Councils "usual working methods are questioned and untraditional thoughts are given place".[21]

Finally, the free commune's experiments have had a broad impact in improving central-local relations and enhancing the case for local autonomy. The number of authorities involved in the experiments may be only a fraction of the total but there has been a substantial spill-over to the remainder of the system. Revised regulations and legislation affecting all authorities have flowed from the schemes. More generally a shift in attitudes and a greater commitment to making local autonomy a reality has occurred. The Swedish Ministry of Public Administration states:

[19] O. Nissen, *Reinforcing Local Autonomy*. Paper presented at the Council of Europe Conference, 28–30 June 1988, p. 6.
[20] The Swedish Ministry of Public Administration, *Free Local Government Experiment in Sweden*, *op. cit.*, p. 19.
[21] Association of County Councils, 1988, *op. cit.*, p. 13.

Through the experiment the dialogue between the state and local authorities has developed and acquired partly new content. A discussion concerning the procedures for state control, local autonomy and democracy, equivalence versus uniformity is now being conducted . . . The dialogue is being broadened and deepened . . . Local autonomy is on the increase.[22]

Conclusions: Some Issues for A British Audience

The actual results of the "free commune" experiment can seem limited. Some of the areas in which the experiments have been developed in Scandinavia are in areas where British local authorities have also experimented, using their discretion without asking the permission of central government. During the 1970s and 1980s British local authorities have extended and enhanced their role in local economic development. Experiments with multi-service decentralised service delivery have been undertaken in a range of authorities. Area-based committees have been established in Basildon, Tower Hamlets and in other areas.[23] These are areas in which British local authorities already had the freedom with which to experiment. What is important, however, is the direction in which the system is moving. The Scandinavian experiments are a strong indication that their systems are moving towards greater decentralisation, which is a very different response from the dominant trend to centralisation in this country. It is true that the British Government in their 1979 White Paper on Controls proposed the abolition of a number of controls, later implemented in the Local Government Planning and Land Act 1980. The controls introduced since then have, however, more than replaced the relatively minor controls then abolished.

The Scandinavian developments are an interesting example of the use of experiments in administrative reform. They use the capacity of a system of local government for diversity and the innovation and initiative that this permits. Experiments can then be a means of governmental learning, the lessons of which can, if appropriate, be applied more generally. The use of private bill legislation once provided a means of experiment and innovation in this country but its use is now more limited. A capacity for experimentation in central-local relations could provide a means of learning within our system. It is, however, important not to see the free local government experiments in isolation. In each Scandinavian country they are part of a wider programme for public service renewal. It is from these overall programmes that this country has most to learn. Too often debates about the role of the market and

[22] The Swedish Ministry of Public Administration *Free Local Government Experiment in Sweden, op. cit.*, pp. 19, 21.
[23] The growth of decentralisation in British local government is indicated by the results of a recent INLOGOV survey. See G. Stoker, F. Wedgwood-Oppenheim and M. Davies, *The Challenge of Change in Local Government. A Survey of Organisational and Management Innovation in the 1980s*, INLOGOV, Birmingham, 1988.

the role of public provision take as their starting point the existing forms of public provision. Slogans of "Defend jobs and services" encourage the assumption that the existing forms of public provision are the only possible form. Scandinavian programmes for public service renewal of which the "free commune" experiments are part, are an attempt to develop new forms of public provision that combine greater responsiveness with efficient service delivery, subject to democratic control.

INDEX

INDEX

expenditure; by local governments,
4–5, 6, 8–9, 10, 14, 29, 69–70, 88;
in Sweden, 127
expenditure targets, 10
experimentation; in administrative
reform, 141
export consortia, 119
EZ *see* Enterprise Zones

Federal Government (West
Germany); and Länder, 97–9, 106
federalism, 45, 62, 87, 97–9
Finance Planning Council (West
Germany), 98
financial autonomy; of local
authorities, 97
financial controls: over decentralised
agencies, 23; over local
government, 8–11, 13, 18–19,
69–70, 71, 87, 88–9
Financial Institutions Group, 33
financial services; for small
businesses, 119
financing of local government, 4–5,
7–8, 9–10, 16, 59, 68–9, 89; in
France, 90–1; in Scandinavia, 128
Finland, 126, 127, 128, 135
flexibility of producers, 114, 120
France: local elections in, 81, 82; local
government in, 82, 85, 86–7; local
taxation in, 90–1
"free communes", 125, 132, 135–8,
140
free market, 28–9

Galt, John, 44
Gamble, Andrew, viii
Gaulle, General de, 86–7, 90
GEAR *see* Glasgow Eastern Area
Renewal (GEAR)
general grant, 4, 6
Gladstone, W.E., 77
Glasgow, 26
Glasgow Eastern Area Renewal
(GEAR), 26, 27
GLC *see* Greater London Council
Goschen, Sir George, 77, 84
Grant Related Expenditure (GRE),
9, 68
grants; to local authorities, 8–10,
13–14, 16, 128

GRE *see* Grant Related Expenditure
(GRE)
Greater London Council, vii, 11, 30,
32, 59, 80
Green Party (West Germany), 96
group self-interest, 57
Gustaffson, Lennart, 132
Gustafsson, Agne, 129, 130

HATs *see* Housing Action Trusts
health services; in Scandinavia, 137,
138, 139
Heseltine, Michael, 9, 72
Hessen, 96, 101, 102, 104
Hessen Land Development Trust
Company, 101
Home, Alec Douglas, Earl of, 55
home rule, 51, 53; *see also* devolution
homosexuality, 61
housing, 6, 8, 17–18, 59–60, 87, 91; in
Sweden, 128
Housing Act, 1980, 59
Housing Act, 1988, 17, 60
Housing Action Trusts, 17–18
"Housing Policy" (Cmnd 6851), 8
Hurd, Douglas, 71

ILEA *see* Inner London Educational
Authority
IMF *see* International Monetary Fund
immigration, 25
incentives to industry, 115
industrial estates, 118, 123
industrial policy: in Italy, 109; in West
Germany, 94, 96, 97–101 *passim*,
103–8
industrial society, 95
industry associations, 101
inflation, 5
information technology, 96, 102
infrastructure, 96, 100–1, 124;
financial, 115–16; social, 110, 120,
123
Inner Area Studies, 25
inner cities, 13, 21, 25, 26, 29, 36
Inner City Enterprises, 34
Inner London Education Authority, 59
Inner Urban Areas Act, 1978, 26
interactive process, 129–30
intergovernmental networks, 78, 84,
86, 87, 88, 90, 91, 92

INDEX